LOOM OF WISDOM

PARABLES AND OTHER STORIES

DR. C.D. VERMA

Copyright © Dr. C.D. Verma
All Rights Reserved.

This book has been self-published with all reasonable efforts taken to make the material error-free by the author. No part of this book shall be used, reproduced in any manner whatsoever without written permission from the author, except in the case of brief quotations embodied in critical articles and reviews.

The Author of this book is solely responsible and liable for its content including but not limited to the views, representations, descriptions, statements, information, opinions and references ["Content"]. The Content of this book shall not constitute or be construed or deemed to reflect the opinion or expression of the Publisher or Editor. Neither the Publisher nor Editor endorse or approve the Content of this book or guarantee the reliability, accuracy or completeness of the Content published herein and do not make any representations or warranties of any kind, express or implied, including but not limited to the implied warranties of merchantability, fitness for a particular purpose. The Publisher and Editor shall not be liable whatsoever for any errors, omissions, whether such errors or omissions result from negligence, accident, or any other cause or claims for loss or damages of any kind, including without limitation, indirect or consequential loss or damage arising out of use, inability to use, or about the reliability, accuracy or sufficiency of the information contained in this book.

Made with ♥ on the Notion Press Platform
www.notionpress.com

Contents

Contents

Preface

The word literature means the body of writing produced in a particular language. It can be classified into three categories: Temporal (secular), spiritual (religious), and psychological. The Hindi equivalent of literature is *Sahitya*. *Sahitya* is of two types: *swanta sukhaiy*, and *parjan hitaiy*. *Swanta Sukhaiy* is that work of art, a book in prose or verse, which is produced for self-pleasure, self-delight and self-satisfaction. *Swanta* means self, and *sukhaiy* means happiness and pleasure. While the *parjan hitaiy* sahitya (literature) has wider connotations. This type of literature is all-inclusive, as it touches the right chord, and brings about a complete metamorphosis in human thinking. It represents benevolence, altruism, and humaneness. In the *Swanta sukhaiy* sahitya falls surrealistic literature or art, or work of pure fiction, of fabrication, such as novels, stories, and anecdotal tales. But in the *Parjan hitaiy* literature fall the writings which appertain the human conduct. Such literature is the outcome of the experiences and observations of life. It provides a stimulus for refining manners and morals. In *Parjan hitaiy,* Sahitya included parables and other didactic stories.

The Ramayana and the Mahabharata are the best examples of *Parjan hitaiy* literature. They are a synthesis of both the temporal (secular) and spiritual (religious) sahitya. They teach us to be "full men," to be "exact men." They have operated upon the psyche of men, and have influenced the "management" of life in a positive way. They are replete with spiritual principles, the moral tenets. In fact, they are dispersed meditations. We learn a lot from them. Parables can be deemed to be part of this type of didactic literature.

In the present volume, have been included parables, both secular and spiritual, as exemplars of *Parjan hitaiy* writings. Parable is denotatively defined as a short story that illustrates a moral attitude, or a religious principle. A parable is, in fact, a temporal story, an earthly story, with heavenly or spiritual overtones. That is why the present book has been given a meaningful title: *LOOM OF WISDOM*. For, the stories cultivate and elevate prudence and sagacity to comprehend the tedious ways of this world.

My daughters, Dr Manjula Batra, and Dr Seema Sharma, both capable academicians, and creative writers, prevailed on me to publish all these stories, tales, and parables in a book form for the general public. Resultantly, here is that book. I am sure that the general readers will not only enjoy the parables and other didactic stories and tales but will also find most of them a welcome addition to their ken.

I am extremely grateful to my daughter, Dr Seema Sharma, who has so diligently seen the book through the press.

Dr. C. D. VERMA
Former Associate Professor and Head,
Department of English,
Hans Raj College, University of Delhi

Introduction

What is a parable? It is a short story that illustrates a moral attitude, or a "religious principle." This is the denotative interpretation. However, the Bible interprets a parable connotatively as a "story in which things in the spiritual realm are compared with the events that could happen in the temporal realm or an earthly story with a heavenly meaning." The Biblical definition, obviously, differs from a fable, myth, allegory, or even a proverb. Nevertheless, it would be erroneous to aver that a parable is a "moral story" with a didactic message. A parable is a kind of apologue. It is a story fundamentally about being human.

An ordinary story can be real or fictional; it can be an imaginary, or maybe an invented tale. But a parable is an integral part of human existence, concomitant to human idiosyncrasies. Life is a journey from birth to death. And, willy-nilly, it becomes a journey from being to becoming. The Indian scriptures call this world as *Bhavsagar*, that is the ocean of life. In this *Bhavsagar*, we move from one dawn to another like a ship cruising in the sea. The sailors in the ship that passes in the night, speak to the sailors in another ship passing at a distance through signal in the darkness. Similarly, in the ocean of life, we pass and speak to one another through "look and voice, which verily represent a "little love, a little hope, and a little dreaming too." There is no wealth as important as life lived purposefully. For the value of life lies not in the length of days, but in the benign and salubrious use we make of those days, for a man may live long, yet live very little.

Shakespeare propounds in "As You Like It" that our whole life is like a play, that we are mere actors in the theatre of life, and that man grows through seven stages of development: First of an infant "mewling and puking in the nurse's arms;" second of a "whining school boy," reluctant to go to school; third of a lover "sighing like a furnace;" fourth of a soldier "quick in the quarrel;" fifth of a justice "full of wise saws and modern instances;" sixth of an aging man, "shrunk shank," his youthful pantaloon, well saved, too wide for his thin and lean body; and in the seventh going into oblivion "sans teeth, sans eyes, sans taste, sans everything."

However, these seven stages can better be explained in modern idioms such as "spill, drill, thrill, kill, bill, ill, and will." A man as an infant spills (corporeal waste); subjects himself to drills (discipline, exercise) in the school; experiences thrills (excitement, titillation) as a youthful lover, writing ballads to his mistress's beauty; tends to kill, like a soldier for the sake of honour and glory; resorts to quote bills (laws, legislation) as a mature wise person occupying a seat of justice (for instance a sarpanch, or a community leader); suffers ills as an infirm, invalid aged person, and finally writes will to bequeath his property to his progenies and goes into oblivion.

Since human nature is immutable, therefore what Shakespeare says is relevant to all times. He is certainly a bard for today. Man passes through this world but once. Any good therefore that he can do, or any kindness that he can show to his fellow-creatures, especially to the aged persons (parents), let him do it now. Let him not defer or neglect it, for he shall not pass this way again. Life is like a tale. How long it is, is not significant. But how good it is, is what matters.

Man is the artificer of his own happiness. If he is firm in his will, he can mould the world to himself and even can tame a tiger. Here is a parable that substantiates this dictum. There lived a hermit in a town. He was famous far and wide for his wisdom and spiritual powers. People thronged to him for advice on personal and domestic problems. Once a housewife came to him and supplicated for help to regain the affection of her husband. She said, "Before he went to war, he was a loving and caring husband. But after his return from war, he has become cold, indifferent, and brawling. Three years' war has completely metamorphosed him into a callous, aloof, and apathetic person." "War does such things to men," retorted the wise wizard.

The woman added: "It is widely acclaimed that you can make a potion which enkindles love in the person who drinks it." She pleaded that she would be grateful if he made such a love-potion for her. The hermit nodded his head in affirmation. "Of course, I can make that potion. But I lack one of the ingredients." "What is that?" asked the lady. "It is a tiger's whisker," replied the hermit. However, he pointed out "where there is a will there is a way."

The woman immediately left for a dense forest in search of a tiger. She eventually came across one. As soon as she neared the predator, the tiger growled. Awed and unnerved, the woman retreated. The next day she again returned to the tiger. The tiger again snarled. The woman did not lose heart. She continued going to the tiger's place time and again. Gradually, the tiger got used to her presence, and stopped growling.

The woman started bringing food for the tiger and soon befriended the ferocious animal. The tiger would come near her and accept food from her hands. She would caress his head and even hug him. One day she timidly plucked one of the tiger's whiskers. The tiger did not react. He was obviously tamed.

The housewife rushed back to the hermit with the tiger's whisker, and presented the same to him with the request to make the love-potion. The hermit took the tiger's whisker and threw it into the fire. The woman was flabbergasted: "What have you done?" she remonstrated. The hermit said that she did not need any love-potion. He commented that through perseverance, patience and a caressing touch, she could tame a ferocious animal like a tiger, and even pluck one of his whiskers. Would a man be less responsive than a savage beast to her balmy, soothing, and tender bearing?

The woman understood the secret of conjugal happiness. She slowly made her way home ruminating over what the hermit had said. When she saw her husband she moved forward with a smile on her face, cuddled his hair, and fondly hugged him. Her husband responded by taking her into his arms. The moral of the parable is that the domestic happiness grows at our own firesides. The spouses need not run here and there in search of conjugal harmony and bliss. There is no gainsaying the fact that parables refine human sensibility, and make us comprehend the real purpose of life.

The Hindi equivalent of literature is Sahitya. There are two categories of Sahitya: one is *swanta sukhaiy,* and the other is *parjan hitaiy.* The former type of literature is meant for self-pleasure, and self-satisfaction, such as novels and other works of fiction, imaginary and invented. While the latter type of Sahitya includes socio-spiritual, qua religious literature, meant to improve the morals and the manners. *Swanta sukhaiy* sahitya is temporal (secular), while *parjan hitaiy* literature is spiritual, such as Indian scriptures, Puranas, and the epics, the Ramayana, and the Mahabharata. Take for example, the Samudra Manthan (Churning of the Ocean), a great mythical event, described in the Bhagavat Purana, the Vishnu Purana, as also in the Mahabharata. It is a profound socio-religious legend, obviously a parable, a didactic story, with symbolic meaning. While it is easy to read the mythical parable as a tale of universal aspiration to achieve immortality, it deciphers analogically the human body and the soul that resides in it. The ocean churned by demigods and demons, represents the mind, or the consciousness, which contains many hidden secrets and treasures. The human body is a microcosm in which reside both the gods and the demigods, just they reside in their respective spheres in the macrocosm. The gods represent the sattva (the purity), the intelligence; they represent virtue, righteousness, and altruism. While the demons represent the evil, sin, delusion, darkness, and grossness of the body. The churning process is, in fact, symptomatic of self-transformation, which metamorphoses the state of temporality to spirituality.

In yet another story, appertaining friendship between Lord Krishna and Sudama, the mythical parable propounds that a friend in prosperity is pleasure, a solace in austerity, and a comfort in companionship. When Sudama, a poor Brahmin, suffering destitution and penury, visits Krishna, the king of Dwarka showers unprecedented warmth and affection on his childhood friend. Rukmini, the celestial consort of Krishna, and an incarnation of goddess Lakshmi, questions her Lord as to why he has showered so much love on Sudama who was guilty of serious transgression, for he had eaten the parched grams clandestinely without sharing the snacks with Krishna as directed by Guru Mata.

Krishna replied that the entire world should be grateful to his friend for this. Sudama ate the grams not because he was hungry, but for a salutary and munificent purpose. He knew that the parched grams were left by the thieves in the Gurukul. He also knew that those grams were stolen from the house of a brahmin woman, and that woman had cursed that who-so-ever ate those grams, he would remain poor throughout his life. So, Sudama ate those grams quietly and stealthily to keep me away from penury. It is because of his sacrifice that I lead a life of plenty and opulence. He had a staunch faith in me, believing that I was the incarnation of Vishnu. And if God incarnate became poor, the whole world would become impoverished. It was a great act of sacrifice on the part of Sudama. He opted for poverty for the benevolence of the entire mankind.

A parable, or say a didactic story, has a special attraction for the intellectual and moral development of mankind. I would prefer to call a parable a benign narrative that adds to the high spiritual principles on the secular side. For the spirit of man is like the lamp of God with which he searches the inwardness of all secrets. Take for example the story "Charity begins at Breakfast Point." A beggar, who would clandestinely slip into the crowd of breakfast eaters, enjoy the breakfast quietly and stealthily, and would go away without making the payment. The owner of the Breakfast Point knows about the trick the beggar plays, but he turns a blind eye and lets the beggar eat the morning fare. When somebody points this out to the owner of the Dhaba, he manifests a highly munificent reaction: "I am convinced that the beggar is the representative of God. He is emblematic of good luck. He comes here much before the customers start coming, sits close to the wall, waits for the crowd to amplify, and through the melee mingles in the swarm of clients, covertly eats the breakfast, and goes away." The owner propounded a salubrious, a spiritual tenet that when the beggar comes in the morning, he prays to God for the crowd of customers to assemble. "His prayer is answered. Resultantly, it fetches me a lot of money every day. I am blessed with plenty owing to the prayer of this man. This is what I believe. And the day he does not come, it becomes a lean day for my business: I only earn a pittance; it turns out to be an unproductive day." What the story, qua the parable, conveys is the fact that "prayer is the voice of faith. More things are wrought by prayer, and by magnanimity, by philanthropy, than this world dreams of."

Yet another story -- "Man Proposes, God Disposes--" signifies that if you insult, humiliate, or batter a sadhu, a holy man, a devout, God would take revenge, and punish the errant knave. Then there is a story entitled "Interview." Its message is loud and clear. Education is not the be-all and end-all of life. Good behaviour and social conduct have greater worth than anything else in life. Parents reprimand wayward and erring children for any act of omission and commission. But their chastisement stands in good stead eventually. For imbibing socio-ethical virtues, one should be grateful to parents, and respect them as mentors and guides.

The stories- "Krishna's Justice," and "Krishna the Diplomat," have the apocalyptic revelation that Krishna, the Supreme Lord, enjoins the denizens of the world to be positive and lovable, and should always follow the path of righteousness and good conduct.

There are many other parables and didactic stories, included in this book, which exude and transmit the same theme, such as God Loves Simplicity and Innocence, *Tale of an Honest School Master, Radha Needs Ghee More than Krishna, Smile Begets Smile, Tale Told by the Buddha, Holy Waters: the Power of Tirtha, Morsel of Human Love, The Power of Guru Mantra, Ursula, the German Friend, When Thakurji Appears as Witness, Charity Begins at Tree, and many other* stories replete with balmy, salutary, friendly and upstanding moralistic overtones. Some of the stories are based on real happenings; they are a blend of facts and fiction.

Suffice to say that we must be the servants and interpreters of Nature. Take the example of a lark that can mount and sing and please herself, and nothing else. But a human being is a different breed. In him, wisdom arrives when he sails through the Ocean of Life (*Bhavsagar*), for the wisdom arises out of the universal insight into the affairs of the world.

Life is not so important as the duties of life, because life is a test, and this world is a place of trial. Life is neither a "good," nor an "evil." It is simply the place where both the good and the evil co-exist. We choose one of the two. Parables help us make the right choice. Life is a jigsaw puzzle with most of the pieces missing. We have to fill the place left vacant owing to the "missing pieces."

"I expect to pass through this world but once. Any good therefore I can do, or any kindness that I can show to any fellow creature, let me do it now. Let me not defer or neglect it, for I shall not pass this way again." Let us subscribe to this aphorism. Let us not live in fragments. Let us "connect" with human beings. This is an altruistic dictum, nay, a "missive" that the present book contains.

Dr. C. D. VERMA

CHAPTER I

Churning of the Ocean: The Symptomatic Reappraisal

(One-Act Play)

CHARACTERS

Vishnu: The all-pervading God
Brahma: The Creator of the universe
Shiva: Mahadeva
Durvasa: The irascible sage
Indra: The chief of demigods
Devas: The demigods
Mohini: Vishnu in disguise of a beautiful damsel
Bali: The king of demons
Vidyadhari: A celestial woman
Gunadhya: The celestial narrator
Lakshmi, Dhanvantri, and others that come out of the ocean churning

PROLOGUE

The Samudra Manthan, that is Ocean Churning (Samudra means ocean and Manthan means churning), is a great mythical event, described in holy scriptures, in the Bhagavat Purana, the Vishnu Purana, as also in the Mahabharata. It is a profound socio-religious legend replete with rich and complex symbolism of the churning of the ocean. In fact, the tale is symptomatic of spiritual India. Most of the people, here and abroad, oriental and occidental, are quite familiar with the main contours of the mythical story. But what is the most significant is not the bland mythical tale, qua the bare facts, but the underlying symbolic meaning. The emblematic undertones are not known much, or less known, to the people at large. While it is easy to read the myth as a tale of universal aspiration to achieve immortality by obtaining amrita (nectar), the myth needs to be deciphered and reappraised analogically vis-à-vis the human body, the soul that resides in it, and the cosmos.

What fomented and engendered the need for ocean churning was an uncanny incident. It was the rage of hot-headed Rish Durvasa, who cursed Lord Indra, for an unsavoury and unpleasant misdemeanour, that he would lose his supremacy over the three worlds.

CURTAIN RAISER

GUNADHYA: My name is Gunadhya. I am a celestial being. I came to the earth in the world of mortals as a storyteller. I was the narrator of tales in Somdeva's *Kathasaritasagara (KATHA-SARITA-SAGARA)*, which is the Ocean of Stories. And I am going to perform the same role of a narrator in telling the story of sage Durvasa, and the churning of the ocean which was necessitated by the sage's anger and curse.

The story of the *Katha-sarita-sagara* opens with Parvati asking Shiva to tell her a tale that she had never heard before. Shiva related the adventures of the Vidyadharas to Parvati. As Lord Shiva narrates the tales of seven Vidyadhara princes, they are overheard by one of the attendants who repeated the tales to his own wife, who happens to be Parvati's door-keeper. This woman, in turn, tells the stories to Parvati who is enraged that Shiva had told her a story that even her door-keeper knew. The erring attendant, Malyavan, is cursed to be reborn on earth as Gunadhya, where he will remain until he has spread the tale he overheard, far and wide. Thus, the story comes to earth and is told to mortals by me, who, actually, is a celestial being.

(Vidyadhara literally means possessors of knowledge. It is a class of inferior deities inhibiting the regions between the earth and the sky, and generally of benevolent disposition. They are attendants of Lord Indra. Yet they have chiefs and kings of their own).

• • •

SCENE: 1

Gunadhya: As aforementioned, I am the first earthly narrator who acts within the story he tells. This provides the perfect point-of-view twist to a complicated myth. The myth has it that Rishi Durvasa had attained spiritual powers through hard penance and meditation. There are many achievements of his life which included significant incidents, pleasant and unpleasant, which moulded the socio-cultural and spiritual annals of India. He is known for his irascible nature. When angry he could curse anyone, mortal or immortal, big or small. Nevertheless, his curses had both good and bad ramifications. Often his victims suffered grave anguish and distress. But, by and large, his curses had eventually salubrious outcome. The Puranas, the Ramayana, the Mahabharata, and other scriptures, are replete with many legends appertaining the sage's curses. He cursed Lord Indra, King Ambrisha, Shakuntla, the wife of Dushyant and mother of Bharata. But from each curse emanated an interesting and significant tale. So much so that his interaction with Kunti, with Draupadi, turned out to be benedictory boons.

The Vishnu Purana, the Vayu Purana, and the Padma Purana, propound that the curse he laid upon Lord Indra, willy-nilly, turned out to be one of the reasons, perhaps the only reason, for the famous churning of the ocean.

SCENE: 2

Gunadhya: Once sage Durvasa was wandering around the world in a state of ecstasy owing to a vow he was observing. Suddenly he espied a Vidyadhari woman (a nymph of the air) who was wearing a beautiful garland of flowers. He addressed the celestial woman:

Durvasa: Devi! You are wearing a heavenly wreath of flowers, out of which is emanating a sweet and pleasing fragrance. Can you give this garland to me?

Vidyadhari: Sage! It is my privilege to give this wreath to a saint of your stature. Here it is.

Gunadhya: Durvasa placed the garland on his head, and continued his journey. On the way, he ran into Indra riding his famous elephant, Airavata. Lord Indra had a train of demigods in tow. Durvasa still in his state of frenzy threw the garland at the chief of gods who caught it and placed it on the head of Airavata. The elephant was surprised at the pleasant fragrance that was coming from his head. He raised his trunk to get a better sniff. In the process, the wreath fell off his head onto the ground.

Durvasa: Indra! How dare you treat my gift with disdain! Instead of placing the garland on your head, you thought it fit to place it on the head of your elephant. The animal shook it down and trampled it with his foot. This uncanny act is a reflection of your arrogance. I must punish you for your delinquent conduct and misdemeanour.

Gunadhya: Indra soon realised his mistake. He got off his elephant, fell at Durvasa's feet, and sought his pardon.

Indra: Sage! I know that I am guilty of my erroneous behaviour. I seek your forgiveness for my dereliction.

Durvasa: No! Nothing doing. Your conduct is unbecoming of your stature, and cannot be overlooked. I, therefore, curse you that you will be cast down from your position of supremacy, of dominance, over the three worlds, just as the garland was cast down.

Gunadhya: Notwithstanding Indra's pleading for forgiveness, Durvasa refused to relent, or soften his curse. As a consequence of the sage's curse, demigods lost their lustre, they became weak. Sages were not performing sacrifices. People had become selfish. The demons became strong. The asuras never liked demigods. There was a perennial struggle between the two. Since Durvasa's curse had debilitated the demigods, the demons seized the opportunity, and under the leadership of Bali attacked the devas, and routed them. The gods fled, and eventually approached Lord Brahma, and sought his protection. But Brahma exhibited his inability to come to their succour. He advised them to go to Lord Vishnu and seek his guidance and assistance, for Lord Vishnu alone could ameliorate their lot.

Devas: Lord Vishnu! We are in dire straits. Sagae Durvasa's curse has weakened us. We are unable to fight against the asuras. We had requested Lord Brahma for help. But he showed his reluctance, and advised us to approach you.

Vishnu: Devas, please listen to me carefully. This is not the opportune time to fight against the demons. It would be in your interest to go for a truce with asuras. I propose that both the demigods and the demons should get together and churn the great ocean. The Mount Mandara should be used as the churner, and Vasuki, the great snake, should be used as a rope for churning. Out of the churning of the ocean would emerge amrita (nectar, that is water of life) that will not only make you eternal but also powerful enough to vanquish the demons.

Devas: And what if asuras also partake in the amrita? They too will become deathless and powerful enough to defeat us in the unforeseen battle.

Vishnu: I assure you that I will plan the strategy in such a way that the amrita will not go to the demons; it will be served only to the demigods. And, thus, the Devas will become immortal.

SCENE: 3

Gunadhya: The demigods acted on the advice of Lord Vishnu. Lord Indra and other gods approached Bali, the king of the demons, and sought his friendship.

Indra: Respected sire, we have come up with a proposal that will make you, me, and other gods and demons, immortal.

Bali: What is that proposal?

Indra: We have been advised by Vishnu, the Supreme Lord, to befriend the asuras. Together we should churn the ocean. From the depth of the ocean will emerge many precious things, including amrita, which we will share with you. Amrita will make all of us, demons and gods, immortal.

Bali: There is a perennial rivalry between gods and demons. We have fought many battles. Why should we trust you that you will share amrita and other *ratnas* with us?

Indra: It is Lord Vishnu who has advised us to approach you and persuade the demons to join the great adventure in the interest of one and all. Please do not doubt our intentions. We have come with a positive mind. And then it is the desire of Vishnu, which you and

I ought to fulfill.

Bali: If that is so, we agree to join you in the churning of the ocean. Please give us your solemn promise that you will share with us Amrita and other things that emerge out of the ocean with us.

Indra: I promise. And assure you that I will stand by my promise.

SCENE: 4

Gunadhya: Eventually the churn began. As directed by Vishnu, devas and asuras uprooted Mount Mandara to use it as a churning rod, and Vasuki, the great snake, who resided on Shiva's neck, became the churning rope. While carrying the massive mountain, several demigods and demons, fell down exhausted; some of them even perished. Lord Vishnu saw their plaintive and disturbing condition. He immediately manifested himself, riding his mount, Garuda, and revived all the devas and asuras, placed Mandara on his mount, and carried them towards the destination. Vasuki coiled himself around the mountain. Then Vishnu advised them.

Vishnu: Devas, please tug the serpent from the head, and let asuras tug it from the tail side.

Demons: No Lord Vishnu! We do not agree with your suggestion. For we suspect your intentions. We will tug the snake-qua the rope- from the head. And let demigods do the same from the tail side.

Devas: We have no problem. Let asuras tug from the head-side.

Gunadhya: The gods were happy with the arrangement. They knew that Vasuki would throw out flames of poisonous fire from his mouth, which would trouble and burn the asuras. Lord Vishnu had deliberately suggested that gods should tug from the head side, because he knew that the demons would remonstrate and pooh-poohed his proposal, and would eventually drag the snake from the head side, and would suffer the poisonous waves, breathed out by the snake. The asuras were poisoned by the fumes that were emitted out of the mouth of Vasuki. Despite that the devas and the asuras pulled back and forth Vasuki's body alternatively, causing the mountain to rotate, which in turn churned the ocean.

Nevertheless, mount Mandara was too enormous, and sank to the bottom of the ocean. Once again Vishnu came to the rescue of gods and asuras. He manifested Himself in the KURMA (Turtle) incarnation and supported the mountain on his back.

During the churning, several wonderful and precious objects sprang out of the depths of the ocean. The first thing that came out of the ocean was a deadly poison (*halahal*). It terrified the gods and the demons because the poison was so powerful that it could destroy all the three worlds.

Gods and Demons: Lord Shiva! You are the healer of all ailments, of all afflictions, of all maladies. Please save us from this lethal poison, which is likely to engulf the entire universe.

Gunadhya: Shiva soon appeared on the scene. To everybody's amazement, he swallowed the poison in one gulp. Parvati, Shiva's celestial consort, who was standing close by, was alarmed by what Shiva had done.

Parvati: My dear Lord! What have you done? I will not let the poison go down your throat.

Gunadhya: Parvati pressed Shiva's neck so tightly that the poison did not flow down into his stomach. Owing to the quick timely reaction and action by Parvati, the poison remained stuck forever in Shiva's throat, neither going up into his mind nor going down into his belly. Since that day, Shiva came to be known as NEELKANTHA, a blue-throated God ('*neel*' means blue and '*kantha*' means throat).

SCENE: 5

Gunadhya: The scriptures propound that the churning of the ocean yielded fourteen *ratnas* (gems, that is precious objects). All the priceless objects were divided between the demigods and the demons. The scriptures propound that there were fourteen *ratnas* that emerged from the Samudra Manthan. According to the quality of the treasures produced, they were claimed by Shiva, Vishnu, sages, the demigods and the demons.

The objects that emanated out of the depth of the ocean, included Poison, the Moon, Kamdhenu (the wish-fulfilling cow),

Kalpvriksh (the divine tree with flowers that never fade), Kaustubha (the most valuable divine gem), Uchhaishravas (the seven-headed celestial horse), Airavata (the white elephant), Panchjanya (Vishnu's conch), Varuni (the goddess of wine), Lakshmi (the goddess of prosperity and wealth), Dhanvantri (the physician of the demigods with the pot of nectar in his hands), and many more ratnas, the precious objects. For convenience, these priceless objects can be divided into three categories. There is a category of goddesses that emerged out of the ocean. They are Lakshmi (the goddess of prosperity and wealth) who is Lord Vishnu's eternal consort. Then there are celestial damsels, called apsaras like Rambha, Menaka, Punjisthala, and others. From the churning also appeared Varuni the goddess of wine. She was accepted by demigods.

Likewise, three types of celestial animals appeared. Kamdhenu, or Surabhi, the wish-fulfilling cow. It was taken by Lord Brahma, and given to the sages to enable them to garner ghee from her milk for the yajnas. Then emerged Airavata, the white elephant. It was taken by Lord Indra. Also emerged Uchhai-shravas, the divine seven-headed horse. This divine animal was taken by Bali, the king of the demons.

Similarly, the ocean churning yielded three most valuable things: Kaustubha, a divine jewel that was claimed by Lord Vishnu; Kalpa-vriksha, a divine wish-granting tree with flowers that could never fade; and Shranga, a powerful bow, given to Lord Vishnu.

In addition to the items aforementioned, the churning produced Chandrama (Moon), which was claimed by Lord Shiva; Dhanvantri (the physician of the devas) with the pot of nectar of immortality.

SCENE: 6

Gunadhya: As soon as Dhanvantri emanated out of the ocean with a pot of amrita, there ensued a great fight between the demigods and the demons for its possession. The demons snatched the pot of nectar from the hands of Dhanvantri, and ran away. The demigods were confused and disheartened. They ran to Lord Vishnu and sought his help. Lord Vishnu appeared in the guise of Mohini, a beautiful and enchanting damsel. She enticed and bewitched the demons, and successfully persuaded them to submit to her mediation and arbitration. The demons agreed.

Mohini: Devas and Asuras, please sit in two separate rows. I will distribute the nectar one by one to all of you.

Gunadhya: Mohini, that is Lord Vishnu, started distributing the amrita in such a way that only gods could partake in it and not the demons. A demon named Rahu, got a whiff of this stratagem. He disguised himself as a deva, joined the row of demigods, and drank some nectar. The sun and the moon found Rahu in disguise. They informed Mohini, who cut off his head with a discus. His body was cut into two parts. From that day the head of the demon was called Rahu, and the body was called Ketu. Thus, all the demons were deprived of the amrita except Rahu who drank a few drops of the nectar and became immortal.

After this, Lord Vishnu abandoned the guise of Mohini, manifested Himself in his original divine form, rode on his mount Garuda, and flew away. Realizing that they have been hoodwinked, the Asuras engaged in combat with devas. Rejuvenated by amrita, the demigods emerged victorious and pushed the asuras to the nether regions (Patala).

This legend is extended further to the origin of Kumbh Mela. While the gods were carrying the amrita away from the demons, some drops of the nectar fell at four different places on the earth, at Haridwar, Prayagraj, Trimbak (Nashik), and Ujjain. These places acquired a certain socio-spiritual significance. A Kumbh Mela is celebrated at these places every twelve years. It is believed that by bathing in the rivers there during the Kumbh Mela, one attains moksha.

EPILOGUE

Samudra Manthan, besides being a great socio-spiritual legend, has significant symptomatic import and connotation. The ocean churned by demigods and demons, represents the mind, or the consciousness, which contains many hidden secrets and treasures. Immortality is also hidden in it. In the scriptures, the mind is always compared to an ocean (*mano sagara*). The ocean also symbolizes *sansara*, which is the phenomenal world (*sansara sagram*). The sages have invariably referred to this world as Bhavsagara, that is the ocean of life, which is flushed with good and bad eventualities, healthy and unhealthy incidents. Just as from the ocean churning emanated both the poison and the nectar, so also every mortal in this phenomenal world is confronted with the good and the bad. And both the good and evil participate in the continuation of the world, qua life. Death is the poison, that is hidden in it. When one churns the ocean, one incurs sinful karma, another poison, which keeps a mortal bound to the god of death. Man cannot resolve both sans divine grace, that is without the help of Lord Shiva.

Furthermore, gods and demons too have socio-religious significance. The human body is microcosm in which reside both the gods and demigods, just as they reside in their respective spheres in the macrocosm. The gods represent the sattva, the purity, the intelligence; they represent virtue, righteousness. While the demons represent evil, sin and delusion (maya), darkness and grossness of the body. And the churning process is symptomatic of self-transformation, which metamorphoses the state of temporality to that of spirituality, of integration of the positive and the negative elements in the human beings. This participation of both the gods and the demons signifies that the mortals seek immortality, and liberation through a spiritual process. They have to integrate and harmonize the subtle and the gross in the human life, qua the world. Every failure or setback, could become an opportunity for improvement and perfection.

There is yet another symbolic significance of ocean churning. It is not merely a physical fact. It is the churning of soul. The soul is the representative of *Parmatma* (God, the Soul Supreme). One may ask what is *Parmatama*? It is an ocean. If you succeed in churning your soul, then from your inside will emerge many ratnas. And for churning the ocean we need Mount Mandara and Vasuki. Mandara is a synthesis of two words, "man" which is mind, and "dara", that is a point, which means a pointed mind in a state of concentration. One cannot practice spirituality, or experience self-absorption without keeping the mind steady. Further, during the churning of the ocean, Mount Mandara was supported by Lord Vishnu in his incarnation as a Tortoise. The Tortoise here stands for *pratyahara*, which is the withdrawal of the mind and senses into oneself, which is essential to practice concentration, meditation or contemplation (dhyana). On the other hand, Vasuki, the divine serpent, represents the resolve, the salubrious desire, the good intention, of gods and demons to obtain amrita and attain immortality. Without the right intention, there can be no initiation into spirituality and no possibility of achieving liberation.

The *halahal* (poison) that comes out of the churning represents the negativity, pain and suffering, anger, pride, doubt delusion, and despair. But when the mind is subjected to intense discipline, and austerities, it throws up negativity and leads to self-purification. Lord Shiva, who swallows poison, symbolizes asceticism, virtue and purity embedded in spiritual life. It is also symptomatic of the divine grace of the Spiritual Master, the Guru. He also represents the ascetic values of renunciation, equanimity, self-control, and self-purification.

Kamdhenu (the wish-fulfilling cow) represents *Pratibha*, that is talent. While Uchhaishrava, the white horse, gives *gati* (motion, momentum, pace) to your resolution and determination. And what you have resolved, eventually reaches its goal with the speed of lightening. Your *Sankalp* (resolve, determination) flies like Pegasus, the flying horse. The emergence of Airavat, the White Elephant, indicates towards the same determination. When you ride an elephant, you get a safe and secure place, unconcerned and undisturbed by the barking dogs. When you rise above your aspirations, you become unconcerned about the barking of the people. You will become *stithpragya* (mental equanimity and stability personified). Your nature, your temperament, becomes balsamic, and you have calm of mind passions all spent. You embark on the journey to achieve your mission in life to elevate yourself spiritually and socially. The Kaustubha, the most valuable gem that emerged from the depths of the ocean, was claimed by Lord Vishnu, who wore it on his head. If one overcomes his aspirations and controls his desires, he will become eligible to get the most precious gem of calmness of mind.

Like Kamdhenu, the celestial cow, Kalpvriksh is also a wish-fulfilling divine tree; whatever one desires, he will get it. And Apsaras (celestial damsels) who emanated out of the sea represent passion, strong erotic passion. And when a man comes out of the claws of passion, then he becomes entitled to things spiritual, including Lakshmi (goddess of prosperity and wealth) and amrita (nectar).

One of the most priceless objects that appeared from the ocean, was goddess Lakshmi. She was gifted to Lord Vishnu. Lakshmi symbolizes material wealth. The act of gifting her to Lord Vishnu, signifies that since all the wealth in the universe belongs to God, it is essential to return to him whatever wealth his devotees, or bhaktas, find or earn in life. His sacrifice will keep him free from karmic debt. According to the Isa Upanishad Brahma is the true inhabitant of the universe, and everything that exists in the universe belongs to Him. One should, therefore, renounce the ownership of wealth and offer it to God. For accumulation of too much wealth and holding on to it, eventually leads to acts unworthy of a noble soul.

And last of all appears Dhanvantri (the physician of gods) with the pot of nectar. He represents health and physical wellbeing, vigour, energy and mental brilliance which emanate out of strenuous austerities, qua penance. Prolonged spiritual practices lead to liberation and immortality.

Lord Vishnu is beyond dualities. He treats everyone equally. In distributing amrita to gods, he did not show any partiality. He simply performed his duty as an upholder of karma and dharma. The Asuras were evil people. No one denied them immorality. They denied it to themselves by their sinful and evil acts and ill-intentions. Vishnu's action signifies the role of God as the upholder of dharma, of good, of righteousness. Therefore, by denying amrita to the demons, He saved the world from their oppression, and thus protected the dharma, the sattvic forces. Mohini symbolizes the power of Maya, who deludes the world, and hinders the process of liberation, and promotes duality, ignorance and desire. Asura owing to their evil nature and demonic qualities, easily fell under the spell of Maya (Mohini), and consequently lost the chance to become immortal, while gods remained focussed on securing immortality, and as such could not be misled by Maya.

The Samudra Manthan has in it an important message that the human life is precious, and that it is through human life that one can attain liberation. Man should cultivate divine qualities to emancipate himself from this Bhavsagara

CHAPTER II

Sudama's Sacrifice for Krishna

(One-Act Play)

CHARACTERS

Krishna: The Supreme God
Rukmini: Celestial consort of Lord Krishna
Balarama: Krishna's elder brother
Sudama: A poor brahmin, and friend of Krishna
Susheela: Wife of Sudama
Sandipani: A sage and Guru of Krishna and Sudama

PROLOGUE

Our birth in a family is under the control of the book of fate. And it is fate that gifts us our filial relations: mother, father, son, daughter, brother, sister, uncle, aunt. But there are two relations we choose ourselves; one is the soul- mate and the other is our friends. There is no gainsaying the fact that friendship is a wonderful relationship, notwithstanding the fact, that it is not bounded by blood, yet it remains more important than the blood relations. And when the friendship is pure and selfless, like the one between Krishna and Sudama, then it is all the more momentous: it assumes the dimensions of a legend.

CURTAIN RAISER

My name is Gunadhya. I am a celestial being. I came to the earth in the world of mortals as a storyteller. I was the narrator of tales in Somdeva's *KATHA-SARITA-SAGARA,* that is the Ocean of Stories. And I am going to perform the same role of a narrator in telling the story of the friendship of Lord Krishna and Sudama, and how Sudama willingly accepted "poverty" to save Krishna from destitution.

It has been enjoined on me by Parvati to perform the role of a narrator and tell stories to the world. Once Parvati asked Lord Shiva to tell her a tale that she had never heard before. Shiva related the adventures of the Vidyadharas (a class of inferior deities, and attendants of Shiva) to Parvati. As Shiva narrated the tales, they were overheard by one of the attendants who repeated them to his wife, who happened to be Parvati's doorkeeper. The woman, in turn, told the stories to Parvati, who was enraged that Shiva had told her a story that even her doorkeeper knew. The erring attendant, Malyavan, is cursed to be reborn on earth as Gunadhya, where he would remain until he spread the tales he overheard. Thus, I continue to perform the functions of a narrator.

$$\bullet \; \bullet \; \bullet$$

SCENE: 1

Gunadhya: The story of Sudama is known to most of the people. But, the significance of the legend is not much known. Sudama was born in a poor Brahmin family, living in Porbandar, a famous town not very far off from Dwarka. His father's name was Matuka and his mother was Rochana Devi. After the Mahabharata war was over, Krishna came to Dwarka, where he built a beautiful city, and ruled there till his death at the hands of a hunter.

The story has it that Sudama and Krishna had a chance meeting in Mathura where Lord Krishna, along with his elder brother, Balarama, had arrived to annihilate Kansa and free the common people from his reign of oppression. While wandering through the town, the duo saw a man, clad in a dhoti-kurta with forehead resplendent in sandal paste. From his exterior, he looked to be a Brahmin.

Krishna: Dau! Look at the beautiful garlands of flowers, out of which is emanating a soothing fragrance. Let us buy some garlands.

Balarama: As you wish.

Gunadhya: When Sudama saw the duo, he at once stood up, and bowed his head before them. He recognised them from their halo as some divinity incarnate.

Sudama: I welcome you, sirs. You seem to be otherworldly. My birth is sanctified to see you. Please order me, your humble servant, whatever you wish.

Gunadhya: Before Krishna and Balarama could say something, Sudama understood what they wanted. He picked up two garlands of fresh fragrant flowers and presented them to the two brothers. Krishna took out some money to pay for the garlands, but Sudama refused.

Krishna: Do you give garlands free of cost to all?

Sudama: Not to all. You are not one among them all. Verily, you are higher than all, rather on the top of all. I am enchanted by the lustre of your halo.

Krishna: If you continue to follow this deleterious practice, how would you keep the wolf from the door?

Sudama: My Lord, you seem to be divinity incarnate. I supplicate to you to treat me as your servant. I place these garlands at your feet.

Gunadhya: Adorned with the blooming garlands, Lord Krishna blessed Sudama with benedictions and walked off. This was just a chance meeting between Krishna and Sudama, which was to accentuate and fructify into friendship later on.

SCENE: 2

Gunadhya: Krishna killed Kansa, and rid the populace of Mathura of his savagery and barbarity. This was the beginning of the victory of dharma over adharma. It is propounded in the Gita that whenever dharma is in danger and the demonic and the unrighteous forces get ascendance over the righteous forces, God descends to the earth to save the world. After having finished his work in Mathura, both the brothers joined the Gurukul of sage Sandipani, for education. The famous Gurukul of Rishi Sandipani was situated in Ujjain. Sudama too was a student there. In Sandipani's ashram, Sudama and Krishna came closer and became great friends. There is a direct reference to this fact in the Bhagwat Purana.

One day, Guru Mata (wife of Sandipani) asked Krishna and Sudama to bring some wood from the forest.

Guru Mata: Krishna, here are some parched grams wrapped in this piece of cloth. If you and Sudama get late while returning, you can eat them to satiate your hunger.

Gunadhya: On the way back to the Gurukul, both the friends were caught in a fierce storm. It rained cats and dogs. They took shelter under a tree overgrown with thick foliage. The pouch of grams was with Sudama. He ate the whole lot without sharing it with Krishna. When Guru Mata came to know about it, she lost the cool of her mind and cursed Sudama that he would suffer penury all his life.

SCENE: 3

Gunadhya: When Krishna, Balarama, and Sudama, completed their education at the Gurukul, they parted ways. Krishna came to Dwaraka, set up a beautiful town there, and ruled over it. But Sudama, a poor Brahmin, led a life of destitution. It was well-nigh impossible for him to make both ends meet. He even could not feed his children. Things came to such a pass that one day his wife, Susheela, thought of reminding Sudama.

Susheela: Dear husband! You and I can suffer hunger. But we cannot suffer the agony of our children; it is our duty as parents to feed them.

Sudama: I too feel pained. But what can be done? We cannot go around the village begging for food.

Susheela: Yes, you are right. But you are forgetting your friend Krishna, about whom you talk so warmly and affectionately day in and day out. You have been telling me that you have a deep bond of friendship with him. He is now the king of Dwaraka. Why don't you go to him? You need not ask him for anything. Your visit to Dwaraka and meeting Krishna might fetch good tidings for our kids. Krishna being an all-knowing all-pervading Lord might ameliorate our dismal condition.

Gunadhya: Sudama agreed to the wise counsel of his wife. He decided to go to Dwaraka. Susheela bound some beaten rice in a piece of cloth and put the pouch in the bag of Sudama. Sudama embarked on the holy pilgrimage to Dwaraka. Yes, it was indeed a pilgrimage for a devotee to a holy place to meet his Lord. After a long tiring journey, he eventually reached Dwaraka.

Sudama: I am amazed to see Dwaraka. What a charming, celestial city! It is built with gold. People appear to be happy and well-provided. And why should it not be so! For it is the city of Krishna's sojourn.

Gunadhya: Sudama asked some common people moving hither and thither about the location of Krishna's palace. When he reached there, he was accosted by the security guard at the gate.

Guard: Who are you? And why have you come here? From your clothes, you seem to be some mendicant. Please go and beg for alms somewhere else. This is the king's palace. You cannot tarry here for long.

Sudama: I am Sudama. I am Krishna's childhood friend. I have come to meet him. Please go and tell Krishna that Sudama has come to meet him. I will be grateful if you oblige me.

Gunadhya: On seeing the attire of Sudama, the guard smirked a bit. However, he hesitantly went in and informed Krishna that one Sudama, claiming to be the King's friend, had come to meet him. On hearing Sudama's name, Krishna immediately stood up and ran to the gate to greet him. Everybody present there, seeing Krishna running post-haste barefooted, was surprised.

SCENE: 4

Krishna: Sudama! O Sudama! My dear friend Sudama! It is after ages that I have seen you. We separated in childhood. How have you been all these long years? Please come in and grace my palace, and add to its glory.

Gunadhya: Once inside the palace, both Krishna and Sudama talked about their days in the Gurukul. Seeing the magnificent stately mansion of Krishna, and the opulence, Sudama felt humble and discomfited owing to his clothes, tattered and ragged. Shattered by his poor condition, he attempted to hide the pouch of rice snacks he had brought for his friend. Krishna espied the discomfiture of

Sudama.

Krishna: Sudama, what is there in this bundle, you are trying to hide? Let me have it. Let me see what is there in it! It must be some gift sent by Susheela, my sister-in-law, for me.

Gunadhya: Krishna snatched the pouch. He opened it and started enjoying the beaten rice. While eating the snacks, he became oblivious to everything else; he was fully immersed in the soothing taste of the humble snacks.

Krishna: What a taste! What a sweetness! I have never tasted such satiating sweetness in my life.

Gunadhya: When Krishna was eating the beaten rice, Rukmini intervened and held Krishna's hand.

Rukmini: Krishna, will you eat and enjoy the sweet rice alone? Please let me partake in them also, and feel the relish and savour of them, and have the feel of blessed delight.

Gunadhya: Krishna smiled his usual winsome smile. He handed over the pouch to his celestial consort. While talking to Sudama, He did not know when he started caressing the feet of his friend. However, Sudama was not aware of it. Being tired of a long journey on foot, and his feet being sore with blisters, the caressing touch of Krishna made him sleep. So engrossed was Krishna in tending his dear friend, that he had become oblivious of everything else, even of the surrounding ambience. Just then Rukmini touched Krishna's shoulders with her hands. Krishna suddenly came up to himself, as if he woke up into reality. He felt a little flustered with a blushful smile on his face.

Rukmini: Lord! I am amazed to see you in this ruminating and reflecting mood. You are the Lord of this world. You care two hoots even for the biggest and the mightiest of monarchs. But as soon as you came to know about the arrival of your friend, Sudama, you became emotional and ran bare-footed to receive him. What is all this?

Krishna: Rukmini, he is my childhood friend. He is my devotee. You won't understand the relationship between me and my bhakta.

Rukmini: But you appear to have forgotten that he had eaten the parched grams alone covertly sans your knowledge, and did not share them with you as was commanded by Guru Mata. Then why did you become so nostalgic and sentimental about him?

Krishna: Rukmini, the entire world should be grateful to my dear friend. He ate the grams not because he was hungry, but for a salutary and munificent purpose for the humanity at large. There is an interesting tale behind it. There lived a Brahmin woman. She was very poor. She sustained her life by begging. Once it so happened that she got a handful of parched grams in alms. While sauntering back home, she got late and reached her hut much after dusk. She did not eat the grams. She felt that she would eat them the next morning after offering a part of them to Lord Vishnu. So, she bound the grams in a piece of cloth and went to sleep.

It so happened that in the night some thieves broke into her house. They searched her hut to lay their hands on something worth-while but could find only a pouch. They groped the pouch and erroneously felt that it contained gold coins. In the meantime, hearing the noise, the woman woke up. She raised an alarm. Her neighbours soon gathered there to apprehend the thieves. But the burglars ran off. They took shelter in the ashram of sage Sandipani. Hearing the hullabaloo, Guru Mata woke up too, and looked for the intruders. Afeared that they might be caught, the thieves left the pouch and made good their escape. When the woman did not find the pouch of grams, she thought that it might have been taken away by thieves. Since the grams could have satiated her hunger, she felt sad, and cursed the pilferers of parched grams: "That whosoever ate these grams, he will face destitution throughout his life." The next day, while cleaning the ashram, the Guru Mata found the pouch of grams abandoned by the thieves. It was this pouch of grams which the Guru Mata handed over to Sudama. He knew that the parched grams were left by thieves in the Gurukul. He also knew that the grams were stolen from the house of a brahmin woman, and that woman had cursed that who-so-ever ate those grams, would remain poor throughout his life. So, Sudama ate those snacks quietly and stealthily to keep me away from destitution. It is because of his sacrifice that I lead a life of plenty and affluence. He had a staunch faith in me, believing that I was the incarnation of Vishnu. Therefore, he was well aware of the fact that if God incarnate became poor, the whole world would become impoverished. Rukmini, Sudama made a great sacrifice for the entire mankind. He opted for poverty for the benevolence of the mortal world. This was an act of great renunciation.

Rukmini: What a sacrifice! What a renunciation! And all this for the amelioration of the human world. I bow before Sudama, your friend and devotee.

Krishna: Now tell me Rukmini, if seeing such a selfless, philanthropic friend, if my heart does not reverberate the feeling of gratitude and love, then what else would make a pulsating human being emotional?

SCENE: 5

Gunadhya: Krishna forced Sudama to remove his tattered clothes, and wear a royal dress. Then both the friends sat to have their meal which was served in gold plates. The Lord of Dwaraka treated his friend lavishly, royally, with much affection. Sudama stayed with Krishna for two days. On the third day, he decided to leave for home, and apprised Krishna of his desire. Krishna agreed. He asked Rukmini, the incarnation of Lakshmi to go and bring Sudama's old clothes which Sudama wore when he came.

Krishna: Sudama, before leaving, please remove the royal robe and wear your old clothes.

Gunadhya: Sudama does as commanded by Krishna. He changes his clothes and then departs.

Rukmini: My Lord Krishna, why have you accoutred Sudama in his old tattered clothes?

Krishna: If Sudama had gone back home wearing the grand regal apparel, people would have sneered at him, giggled at him, that he got rich gifts from Krishna his royal friend. This banter, this derision, would have hurt his self-respect. He would have felt humiliated; he could not have gone back to the same state he came from. Dressed in his old clothes, he would escape the public opprobrium, the critical censure. What I have given him is just the meagre requital for his devotion to me; so much love and care I have for my devotee (bhakta).

EPILOGUE

A friend is in posterity a pleasure, a solace in austerity, a comfort in grief, and a joy in companionship. What is a friend, one may ask? It is a single soul which dwells in two bodies. And the friendship between Krishna and Sudama substantiates all the aforementioned aphorisms. This friendship is replete with many a socio-cultural resonance.

Krishna acquitted himself well in his friendly obligations. When Sudama returned home, he did not know that a great surprise was waiting for him. In place of his dilapidated home, he saw a big palace. Initially, he thought that some big landlord might have acquired his place and built a mansion there. But when he saw his wife and children coming out of the mansion, he was surprised. Verily, this was an example of true friendship. Sudama's wife averred: 'Look at Krishna's might. We have been rid of poverty. Lord Krishna has ended our miseries.' Sudama recollected Krishna's benedictions; tears of gratitude welled out of his eyes. The story of Krishna and Sudama teaches us the real value of friendship. We should not demand anything in reciprocation for our devotion, our bhakti for God. God knows everything. He creates a better plan than what we envisage.

CHAPTER III

The Interview

Ram, now a callow young man, has been a brilliant student, right from his school days. He hails from a sanctimonious family believing in the values of life, and the traditional filial ethics and conventional social norms. His father, a strict disciplinarian, did his best to bring his son up in the best tenets of ethical virtues.

After having done his graduation in commerce, he has been strenuously seeking a job, but without any tangible outcome. At last, one day he got an interview call for a job in an office. He woke up early in the morning, got ready, and hired a three-wheeler to reach the interview place.

On the way, he mused that if he succeeded in the interview and got the job, then he would abandon his ancestral house where he lived with his parents in the village, and shift to a house in the city. And this will help him escape the daily admonition and rebuke that he got from his father for even minor acts of omission and dereliction. He thought that right from the morning when he woke up till late in the evening, "My father chastises me even for small lapses. For instance, after I get up, my father commands me in his garrulous voice to change the bed sheets and the pillow covers, and set the bed in order." Then comes another order: "Go to the bathroom and have a hurried shower. Don't occupy the wash-room for long, for others have to use it too. Make sure that you do not leave the tap running; shut the tap-knob tightly before you leave the wash-room." It is true that in the hurry and skurry quite often the tap is left loosely tight, and thus leaking. Then comes another dressing down. "Spread the wet towel outside on the wall to dry up." And all these commands have to be followed without grumbling.

After breakfast, when I get ready to go out, there comes yet another scolding. "Have you switched off the fan and the light?" These reprimands are a daily routine. "Perhaps I am taken to task throughout the whole day as I do not do any work, partly because I am jobless, and partly because I am sluggish and lack the ability to do anything. I, therefore, pray to God to bless me with a job and save me from the daily brouhaha, nay hoo-ha and furore. I will leave my parents and settle in the town away from daily rebukes and chastisements."

He was still ruminating when he reached the office premises. There he saw many other candidates sitting on the benches and waiting for the interview to start. It was about 10-30 AM. Ram suddenly espied that the light in the office was still on. He immediately recalled the reprimand of his father, got up and switched off the light. Then he noticed that the water from the water cooler was leaking and "drip-dropping." He remembered the snub of his mother, again got up and tightened the tap to stop the leaking water. Then he saw a board hung on the wall on which was written that the interview would take place upstairs on the first floor. Ram started climbing up the stairs. He suddenly saw the light burning on the stairs. He switched off the light and sauntered ahead. There was a chair hindering the passage to climb upstairs. He removed the chair for the convenience of those climbing up, or coming down the stairs. He too sat on a bench like many others who were sitting there and waited for his turn.

He noticed that the candidates went in and came out fast as if they sprinted across. On enquiry, Ram found that the boss did not ask any questions, and let each one of them leave without subjecting them to any questions or queries. When Ram's turn came, he went in, greeted the boss, and placed the file containing his bio-data before the interviewer. But the boss returned the file without looking into it. He did not scrutinize, nor appraise his testimonials. He only looked at Ram's face intently. Then asked; "When can you join your duty?" The question flabbergasted Ram a bit. His initial reaction was that perhaps the boss was joking. Then looking straight into Ram's eyes, the boss said: "Don't feel perplexed and mystified. I am speaking the truth. In today's interview, I did not ask any question to anybody. I only looked at the CCTV and observed and discerned all that was happening outside in the waiting room. Everybody came but nobody switched off the light, nor stopped the water leaking from the tap of the water-cooler. You did that. You removed the chair from the way to the stairs. Blessed are your parents who have brought you up in such emulating manners, and taught you good, responsive, ethical manners, and social conduct. Obviously, you have imbibed such virtuous traditions and habits and propensities. One who does not have a wealth of self-discipline, howsoever smart and intelligent he may be, he always lags behind in the race of life, nor can he manage life properly, for life is a jigsaw puzzle with most of the pieces missing. Such a man would never succeed in life."

The words of wisdom of the boss gladdened Ram's heart. After the interview, he rushed back home and touched the feet of his mother and father. When his father came to know that his son had got the job, he hugged him warmly. Ram forgot all the temperamental outbursts of his father, and his irritations at his reprimands. For Ram, the chastisements of his father stood in good stead. From the reprimands, he at last learnt that what was more precious in life was socio-ethical wealth which eventually proved to be more valuable than the degree he earned from the university. A belated realization dawned on him that education was not the be-all and end-all of life. Good behaviour and social conduct were more significant than anything else in life. Ram felt: "With the socio-ethical demeanour that he willy-nilly inherited from his father and mother, helped him acquit well in life. For leading a happy life, good conduct and manners are imperative, and for imbibing these virtues, respect for parents is essential. Both the father and the mother inculcate in sons and daughters a desire to live a life of self-discipline.

CHAPTER IV

Charity Begins at Breakfast Point

Close to my house, in the flourishing market, there is a small but well-embellished restaurant. On the large board, placed in front of the eatery, is written in bold letters: "BREAKFAST POINT." Whenever I got late for my breakfast at home, I used the pretence that I was getting late for my college. In fact, the ruse has been a subterfuge to relish the hot, enticing, sumptuous fare at the Breakfast Point. The breakfast Point has been so popular that there always was a swarm of breakfast eaters. Like many others, I too waited for more than half an hour for my turn.

One day something strange happened. When I reached the Breakfast Point, I saw a beggar sitting at a little distance away from the restaurant. When, a little later, the crowd of the breakfast eaters proliferated, the beggar slipped into the throng quietly, ate the breakfast, and went away without making payment. I saw all this, but did not think it proper to bring it to the notice of Dyalu, the owner of the Breakfast Point.

A couple of days later, I again stopped at the Breakfast Point. When I reached there, I did not find much crowd. However, I saw the same beggar sitting quietly at about a distance of a hundred meters, and looking with riveted eyes at the *dhaba*. As time passed, the crowd swelled, and there was quite a melee. The beggar got up, sauntered towards the Breakfast Point, silently waded through the swarm of people, tip-toed close to the breakfast counter, ate the food to his fill, and then walked away without paying anything to the restaurant owner.

But I ignored what I saw, notwithstanding the fact, that Dyalu, the owner of the Breakfast Point and I had developed quite a close acquaintance. Nevertheless, I did not feel it proper to complain against the beggar to the owner of the eatery. However, a few days later, I again saw the same beggar using the same trick, a routine that he invariably espoused. This time, I could not control my indignation. I walked up to Dyalu and whispered into his ears about the chicanery the beggar committed clandestinely. Dyalu conveyed his reaction in a hush-hush tone: "Please don't get uneasy. I will talk to you later. Let the beggar have his food undisturbed, and leave as usual."

After the beggar had left, and the crowd had thinned a little, I asked Dyalu: "Why did you allow the beggar to leave without making the payment for the fare?" I was amazed to hear the reply of Dyalu. The revelation he made was an eye-opener, a sort of awakening for me. He said: "I know about the beggar eating the breakfast gratis. You are not the only one to tell me about this. Many others have brought this happening to my notice, but I ignored all the complaints. Now I tell you the secret. This beggar is an asset to me, rather a boon, a blessing in disguise. He comes to the Breakfast Point as soon as I open it. He sits there at a distance, waits for the customers to come, and when there is quite a swarm of people enjoying the breakfast, he meekly and quietly glides through the crowd, satiates his hunger, and saunters out. He thinks that his action of ingress and egress in the crowd has escaped notice. But it is not so. People watch him, notice his actions, and eventually tell me about his surreptitious venture. But I have always turned a blind eye and a deaf ear to what he does. I have never uttered any harsh word to hurt him; nor did I ever insult or humiliate him. Willy-nilly I am convinced that he appears to be a representative of God, emblematic of "good luck." He comes here much before the customers start arriving, sits there close to the wall, waits for the crowd to amplify, and through the melee, he slowly walks and clandestinely eats the breakfast, and goes away quietly."

Dyalu, the owner of the Breakfast Point then came out with a spiritual tenet. He opined: "When the beggar comes in the morning, he prays to God for the crowd of customers to assemble for breakfast, and this fetches me a lot of money every day. I am blessed with plenty owing to the prayer of this man. This is what I believe. And the day he does not come, it becomes a lean day; what I earn is meagre. Literally, it turns out to be an unproductive day." The owner, Dyalu, further added: "Professor! Now you know Why I don't restrain, and inhibit, the beggar from taking breakfast free of cost. I am convinced that if ever I dare stop him, it would amount to self-imposed financial loss. I would not like to mutilate my serendipity, my own fortune. Therefore, I would never stop him. Let him have his breakfast unhindered. Verily, prayer is the voice of faith; more things are wrought by prayer than this world dreams of. For prayer is a blessing in disguise. For most people: "charity begins at home," but for me, it begins at my "Breakfast Point."

"I was hungered, and you gave me meat; I was thirsty, and you gave me drink; I was stranger, you took me in." The Biblical (Matthew: xxv: 35) aphorism contains a perennial message for the human beings at large. "There is no gainsaying the fact that the things you do for yourself are gone when you are gone, but the things you do for others remain as your legacy," finally opined Dyalu. As is implied in his name, he is certainly "Dyalu," an altruistic, compassionate, humane human being.

CHAPTER V

Krishna's Justice

Whatever we do, we think that we have done the best. But whether the deed is right or wrong, who will decide? Obviously, it is the omnipresent and omniscient God, qua Lord Krishna, who judges the intention behind every errand, big or small, especially when it is an act of munificence, kindness and goodwill; and it is God who decides the reward accordingly.

Once it so happened that two close friends, Gopal and Mohan, were sitting on the stairs of a temple. They were gossiping, joking and giggling. Suddenly, the sky was overcast with dark clouds, and the ambience turned into twilight. The friends moved inside the temple. It was close to afternoon, and lunchtime. Just then another man, deterred by the worsening weather, came there and took shelter inside the temple. He too sat with the two friends and joined Gopal and Mohan in a tete-e-tete. A little while after that, the third man, named Vishwas, said that he was feeling hungry. The duo too said that it was time to take lunch.

Mohan took out a packet from his bag. He proposed: "Friends, I have three chapatis, which we can share between the three of us." However, Vishwas added: "I have five chapatis. Together they come to eight chapatis; three plus five." Vishwas proposed that they should divide the eight chapatis equitably, and eat them. But they were confronted with a puzzling predicament as to how to divide eight chapatis among the three equally.

Gopal, the eldest among the three friends, appeared to be sagacious. He suggested that they should slice the eight chapatis into three pieces each. "And in this way, we shall have three into eight, that is 24 pieces, in toto. Accordingly, the three of us will have eight pieces each. And this will come to equitable and proportionate distribution of the fare available.

Soon the gloom of the dusk overtook them. Their hunger having been appeased a little, they went to sleep in the temple itself. They got up early in the morning as soon as it dawned. However, Gopal, the eldest among them, had woken up much earlier. He eagerly waited for Mohan and Vishwas to get up. He wanted to compensate them for the noble deed of feeding him, as he partook in the chapatis of both Mohan and Vishwas. As soon as Mohan and Vishwas woke up, Gopal gave them eight coins of gold. After that, he sauntered out of the temple without uttering a word. Then Vishwas suggested that they should divide the eight gold coins among the duo and take four coins each.

However, Mohan pooh-poohed the very idea, saying that it would be an act of greed and selfishness and that they would be arraigned for hoodwinking a friend. However. Vishwas paid a deaf ear to Mohan's objections. Nevertheless, Mohan eventually acquiesced and yielded before the cogent arguments of Vishwas. He, then, proposed that since he contributed three chapatis, he would take three gold coins. And Vishwas should take five coins as he contributed five chapatis. Then ensued a heated exchange of words between the two. In order to get the riddle solved, they approached the temple priest, and sought his help to settle the dispute.

After having heard the problem the two friends faced, the priest advised them: "Don't quarrel. Let Lord Krishna solve the predicament. Leave these eight coins with me. Let me ruminate over the problem. I shall come out with the solution tomorrow morning." The two friends agreed. They handed over the eight coins to the priest. The priest pondered over the matter and tried various solutions to solve the riddle, but could not arrive at any tangible solution. He then went to sleep. While he was in a deep sleep, Lord Krishna appeared in his dream. The priest narrated the whole story to the Lord, and sought his guidance. However, the priest gave his own suggestion that three-plus-five division as proposed by Mohan, appeared to be just and justifiable.

Lord Krishna smiled his usual winsome smile, and said: "No! Your solution is inequitable, unjust and unfair. Mohan who contributed three chapatis, should get one coin, and Vishwas should get the remaining seven." The priest was flabbergasted. He asked: "Lord! How can that be? It would not be equitable and proportionate distribution of the gold coins." Lord Krishna smiled again. "Look! Mohan did nine pieces of his three chapatis. And out of nine, he ate one piece and shared the remaining eight pieces with his two friends. Therefore, his sacrifice was only one piece. Thus, he should get only one coin, his rightful claim. On the other hand, Vishwas divided his five chapatis into fifteen pieces (five into three), out of which he ate eight pieces, and the remaining seven he divided among his two friends. Accordingly, he has the right to seven coins. This is my arithmetic. And this is my justice."

The priest bowed his head before Lord Krishna for the just and justifiable decision. Verily, our comprehension, qua our judgment, vis-à-vis a problem, is different from that of God. We are unable to understand God's justice. Normally, we eulogize one sacrifice sans our abilities. But Lord Krishna compares our sacrifices, our capabilities, to our actions. It is not important how much wealth we have garnered, or how much significant our sacrifice is! What is vital, what is consequential, are our acts of charity, of munificence. So, "let us be happy, be positive and be lovable."

CHAPTER VI

Krishna, the Diplomat

Once it so happened that Lord Krishna was standing in front of the mirror, and dressing himself up. He was trying different crowns on his head. Sometimes he would put on a crown made of gold bedecked with precious jewels, and sometimes a crown made of silver, equally shining and garnished with multi-coloured pearls and gems of rare beauty. After having put on the crown of his choice, he started dressing himself in various robes, sparkling and shimmering. He took much time in embellishing himself. All this while, his charioteer waited outside at the exit gate with chariot ready, yoked with sturdy steeds. The chariot looked spic and span.

The charioteer thought that Krishna was generally punctual. He never got late for any official or diplomatic errand. But on that day the charioteer was flabbergasted a bit as to what made his master late. To set his curiosity at rest, he went inside to find out if the programme of Krishna to go out was still on, or if he had changed it. For he thought that the mood of Krishna was unpredictable and ambivalent. He could change his schedule at any time. When the charioteer peeped into the dressing room, he found Krishna standing in front of the mirror, trying different crowns and attires. Thus accoutred, he appeared to admire himself.

The charioteer, being the confidant of Krishna, went in, and dared ask: "My Lord, why are you dressing up so much today, and taking such a long time? Where are you going? Is it some special place, and some special occasion, or ceremony?" "I am going to meet Duryodhana," replied Krishna. The charioteer got confused a bit at the reply of Krishna. "Are you dressing up so much with precious jewels and accoutrements just to meet Duryodhana?" Lord Krishna was quick to set the curiosity of the charioteer at rest. "Yes! I am adorning myself so much only for him, for Duryodhana cannot discern what is there inside me. He can only appreciate the exterior ostentation, the outer façade. Therefore, I have flourished myself extravagantly to impress him, for he has closed the eyes of his mind to see the beatific rapturous bliss I hide inside."

The charioteer, loyal and dutiful as he was, respectfully advised his master: "Lord Krishna! It does not behove you to go to Duryodhana. Rather he should come to you. I dare not accept this kind of diplomatic protocol. This is not fair. Look at your status! And look at him; he is too small before you. You are the Lord of the world. And he is just a mortal with all the characteristic faults and idiosyncratic infirmities. Therefore, you should not go to him. Instead, let him come to you. I reiterate and insist on my opinion."

Lord Krishna turned back, looked at the charioteer, smiled his usual captivating smile, and said: "Darkness does not come to light. Light has to go to the darkness. The first thing God created in the world, was the light of the senses; the last was the light of the reason, and ever since then has been the illumination of the spirit." The charioteer bowed his head before the Lord and said that He was right, and on the path of righteousness. Krishna embarked on his diplomatic mission to accost Duryodhana. The rest is history, the apocalyptic revelation.

CHAPTER VII

God Loves Simplicity and Innocence

It is an interesting story, a didactic one, of Sadhu Ram, a pure simple person, straight and upright. He had no ill-will against anyone, no rancour or base thoughts. He lived in a thickly populated village. He did nothing and had no work to do. His family generally pooh-poohed his idleness. What was the most irritating to his family was that he was a voracious eater. His food intake was unusual. He would eat and eat. Since he had no work, he would sprawl on the bed, loll and lounge in the house, all day long. If his mother, or father, requested him to do some domestic work, such as bring groceries, or vegetables, from the market, he would always turn a deaf ear to do any errand on one pretence or another. Eventually, everybody in his family-- his father, his mother, his brothers and sisters – got so sick and fed up that they turned him out of the house. But he did not mind his being driven out. In fact, his eviction from his home and hearth had little effect on him. His only worry was food.

After having been expelled from home, Sadhu Ram, as implied in his name, came to the temple situated in the closest proximity of his house, and sat at the stairs. There he saw some saffron-clad mendicants inside the temple. All of them looked healthy and well-fed. Just then the head priest asked Sadhu Ram as to why he was sitting at the stairs of the temple. Sadhu Ram, a simple and innocent person as he was, said that his family had turned him out of the house. When the priest asked him, "Why?" he replied that he did not do any work and that besides his idleness and sluggishness, he was a voracious eater of food, which his parents resented and asked him to leave the house.

The head priest, a highly religious man, popularly called Guruji, manifested his compassion by caressing his head. He said: "You can stay in the temple as long as you wish, and you don't have to do any work." Sadhu Ram, impressed by the priest's affection, requested: "Guruji, make me your disciple, and let me stay in the temple like other ascetics." Guruji agreed. However, he gave him a pious errand: "Sadhu Ram, as is implied in your name, you are destined to live in a temple. The only work you have to do, is to serve the deities, and the inmates living here. As regards food, there is no dearth of it. Eat as much as you can."

Guruji anointed Sadhu Ram as his disciple and presented to him a rosary made of Tulsi wood to wear. And also whispered the sacred mantra into his ears. He told Sadhu Ram: "You don't have to do any work except the daily routine of oblations and prayers in propitiation of the deities in the temple. Besides, you will serve the inmates and other fellow disciples. So, no work. Only chanting Ram! Ram! And pooja of gods. You can eat food not twice, but even thrice, or four times a day."

Sadhu Ram ruminated: "How nice is it? No work, much to eat, and sufficient space to relax and sleep." So, he decided to stay in the temple, and not to aspire to go home, even to meet his kith and kin. He had been living in the temple for a few days, when one day he confronted a predicament. After being free from his daily routine of oblations, prayers and worship, he saw that there was no flurry in the temple, there was no commotion, only silence. Everybody was relaxed; no preparation for food. Sadhu Ram, a glutton, having an unsatiable urge for food, felt distraught to learn that on that day no food would be prepared. Those who were engaged in preparing the food, were sitting and relaxing on the benches. He approached Guruji to know as to why food was not being prepared on that day. Guruji told him: "It is the day of *Ekadasi*, and on *Ekadasi* (the eleventh day) everybody keeps fast. And as such no food would be prepared today." Sadhu Ram was shaken out of his complacency-- nay stupefied a little. It was, literally, a bolt from the blue. He told Guruji that he "could not live without food. And if he did not get food on *Ekadasi*, he would not see *Dwadasi* (twelfth day)."

However, Guruji proposed that if the food was so essential for him, then he should prepare it himself. Since Sadhu Ram had no alternative except to accept the proposal of Guruji, he requested that he be given a ration – flour, pulse, vegetables, sugar, etc. – so that he could prepare the food for himself. Guruji asked him to go and get the food items he required from the store. Acting accordingly, Sadhu Ram took two kg of flour, potatoes, salt, condiments, ghee and so on. Nevertheless, Guruji advised Sadhu Ram that before taking the food, he must offer a part of it to God. He said: "Alright." He collected the food items hurriedly and sauntered towards the rivulet to prepare the food in an isolated place without being disturbed by anybody. He sat down at the bank of the rivulet, collected the wood from the jungle, ignited the fire, and prepared sufficient food for himself. Being a novice, he cooked the fare in whatever way he could. Earlier he ate the food prepared by expert hands. But today it was a different day.

After having prepared the food, he recalled the command of his Guruji that before eating, he should offer a part of the food to God. Sadhu Ram was so simple that he started calling God: "Lord Rama! Please come soon, and partake in the food prepared by me with my own hands, and drink the cool, pure water of the stream, shimmering in the zephyr." But Rama did not manifest himself. Sadhu Ram reiterated his supplication: "Lord Rama! I know it is simple food. But it has been prepared by your devotee. It is puree and *chokha*. But there are no sweets. There is no tap water. Instead, it is the stream-water. Whatever simple and meagre food is available, it may not be well cooked, but it has been cooked by a simple and innocent heart. Please come soon, and share it. If you don't come, I will also not eat the food."

Sadhu Ram further said: "I know that you are used to getting the sumptuous food items in the temple. But today is *Ekadasi*, and there is no food prepared in the temple. Therefore, whatever food I have prepared is the available fare for today. So, you will have to make do with this simple food. Do come soon! Don't be late! I am feeling hungry." Sadhu Ram spoke simple words to solicit the presence of Rama. Eventually, Lord Rama was pleased with the purity of heart of his devotee, his simplicity, and his child-like innocence.

He immediately manifested himself along with his celestial consort, Devi Sita. When Sadhu Ram saw that instead of one, there were two deities, he was perplexed. He felt that he had invited only one God, but there were two, Rama and Sita. He ruminated that if he fed both of them, there would be no food left for him. But he soon reconciled to the situation and requested both of them to sit and have the ordinary food.

When Rama and Sita were having the food, Sadhu Ram looked at both of them with eyes constantly riveted at the celestial halo and beatitude personified by both the deities. He was elated to see the manifestation of the divinity sitting in front of him. He became oblivious to his hunger. He only wallowed in the heavenly seraphic lustre, glittering and sparkling. He was morose a little that Guruji had told him about one Bhagwan (God), but there were two. He would look at the divine beings and then at the food alternatively. Nevertheless, he thought that since the two deities instead of one, had come, so he must serve them. He requested: "Lord Rama, since you have come with Mata Sita, please sit here and have the food." Rama and Sita had the fare. Sadhu Ram was so simple and innocent a person that he presumed that after the deities had the food, some food would still be left for him to eat on the day of *Ekadasi*. Lord Rama, all-knowing God, read his mind. He left a part of the food for Sadhu Ram with which he satiated his hunger a little bit.

He said, notwithstanding the fact that he remained half-fed, "I am elated to see you." Next time, I will make arrangements for a greater quantity of food. But don't make me wait. Come soon." Ram said: "OK, I will not make you wait. I will come as soon as you summon me."

Thereafter, Sadhu Ram returned to the temple. When his Guru enquired, he did not narrate the actual and whole story. He told his Guru that he prepared the food, and offered a part to God, who came and relished the prasad. "What was left was eaten by me." A few weeks later came another day of *Ekadasi*. He requested Guruji to increase the quantity of the ration as instead of one God there came two. The Head Priest thought that he must have remained hungry. So, he allowed him to have as much ration as he desired. Thus, he got provision for three persons, Lord Rama, Sita and for himself. Instead of two kg, he got three kg of flour and similarly other items in the increased proportion. As before, he repaired the rivulet, collected the wood, ignited the fire, and prepared the food for three persons. Then he chanted: *"Raja Ram aieye, Sita ko Saath laieye"* (come Raja Ram, and bring Sita along with you). Soon Lord Rama appeared. But this time, instead of two, there were three deities, Rama, Sita and Lakshman. When Sadhu Ram saw that instead of two, there were three celestial beings, he was baffled and mystified, because he had food for three persons, but there were four now. He was aghast to think: "This is a strange God. Solicit one God, but come two; invoke the presence of two deities, thee come three." He simply asked Rama: Lord! "Who is this third person?" Rama said: "He is my younger brother, Lakshman." Sadhu Ram, simplicity personified, argued: "He does not appear to be your brother, for he does neither resemble you in countenance, nor in demeanour." Rama reiterated: "No! No! He is my younger brother indeed." "Well, I accept what you say," added Sadhu Ram. "But why do you think that I am saddled with the burden, nay the liability, to feed the whole family of Thakur Ji? Guruji had commanded me to first offer a part of the food to God. He told me about one God. First, two deities come, and now the number has proliferated to three." Lord Rama had a hearty laugh at the simplicity of Sadhu Ram. And so did Sita.

Annoyed at the audacity of Sadhu Ram, Lakshman interjected; "Bhaiya! To what a strange place you have brought me? This man is questioning my appearance and comportment. Obviously, I am not welcome here." Hearing this disparagement from Lakshman, the simple and innocent Sadhu Ram apologised for his impudence. Nonetheless, he was ecstatic to see the three divinities bedecked in celestial sheen. Then, he importuned the trio to sit and have the food. After they had finished eating the fare, Sadhu Ram, like a zealot devotee, with tears wallowing out of his eyes owing to a feeling of thankfulness, sprawled prostrate at the feet of Lord

Rama, and humbly asked: "Lord! Please tell me in advance as to how many of you would come on the next day of *Ekadasi*, so that I may make the provision for food accordingly That is my only worry. Otherwise, there is no problem." Lord Rama did not specify the number; He only said that they would come in time next time.

On the day of the next *Ekadasi*, Sadhu Ram appeared to be depressed and dejected. Guruji asked the reason for his sadness and despondency. Sadhu Ram replied: "There many people come; not one, not two, but three. And who knows next time how many deities would come?" He requested for seven KG of flour and other items in a proportionate quantity. Guruji thought that he could not consume that much ration alone; he must be selling a part of it. When Sadhu Ram left for the banks of the rill as before, the Head Priest followed him walking behind him at a distance stealthily.

Sadhu Ram, the devotee of Lord Rama, was a unique person, out of the ordinary. His actions and reactions were inexplicable. When he reached the rivulet, he kept all the items of the ration under a tree. He neither collected the firewood, nor ignited the fire, nor did he prepare the food. He thought that first, he should see as to how many deities would come. Then, in accordance with the number of persons, he would prepare the food. He, then, vociferously solicited: "*Raja Ram aieye, Sita Ram aieye, Lakshman Ram aieye*, to partake in the fare I have prepared." In response to the call of his staunch devotee, Raja Ram appeared along with "full Ram Darbar," Rama. Sita, Lakshman, Bharat, Shatrughan and Hanuman. Sadhu Ram uttered a cry of joyous exhilaration: "Jai Ho, Raja Ram. This time you have come with the whole brood of kith and kin. Besides, you have brought Hanuman, your trusted devotee."

Seeing all of them, Sadhu Ram, announced; "I must make it clear. When I called one, came two. And when I invited two, came three. And now comes the entire family, the whole Ram Darbar. Please listen to me carefully. I have not prepared the food. There lies the ration. Prepare the food yourself, and eat." Rama asked, "why didn't you prepare the food?" Sadhu Ram answered: "Why should I prepare the food when I have not to get it, and remain hungry?

Today, you have crossed all limits. Besides, several relations, you have brought a monkey too." Lord Rama smiled his usual winsome smile. He requested Sita, Lakshman and others that the wish of his devotee, of his *Bhakta*, was sacrosanct to him. "Let us prepare the food," Rama ordered Lakshman to sit under the tree. Bharat was asked to collect firewood from the jungle. Hanuman cleaned the whole space with his tail. Sita was given the task of preparing purees, halwa and *chokha*. Seeing all the deities thus engaged in preparing the food, many demigods and sages descended on the scene. All of them said in unison: "Mata Sita! We should also get *Prasad*." Sadhu Ram sat there quietly with eyes closed. He presumed that when he was not to get food, then why should he see it being prepared?

After some time, he opened his eyes. He was wonderstruck to espy that many demigods and Rishis, were sitting there in a line, and waiting for the prasad, being prepared by Devi Sita and Lakshman. When the food was prepared, Bharat started serving it. In the meantime, Guruji, who had registered his presence, saw that his disciple was sitting quietly. When Sadhu Ram saw Guruji, he asked his preceptor to come and see "how many deities, demigods and sages, you have set after me." Guruji replied: "I don't see anybody except you alone." Bhagwan smiled. But Sadhu Ram wept. He felt that Rama had put him in another trouble: "Guruji could not let him eat food on *Ekadasi*, while Lord Rama is having food on *Ekadasi*. And yet He is invisible." He solicited Rama to manifest himself to Guruji too. Lord Rama whispered in the ears of Sadhu Ram that He would not give darshan to his Guruji. Sadhu Ram was flabbergasted. He asked: "Lord! Why would you not manifest yourself to Guruji? He is my Guruji, my preceptor. It is he who has guided me to reach you. He is really great."

Lord Rama agreed that there was no doubt about the greatness of your Guruji. "He is exceptional, wise, a noble soul and a spiritual being. He is a man of calibre and reputation. And yet I would not manifest myself to him. I have given you divine eyes to see me." Sadhu Ram asked: "Why Lord?" Bhagwan said: "Your Guruji has all positive qualities. He imbibes all the characteristics of a humane human being. Despite all this, he will not see me." Sadhu Ram again said: "Why?" Bhagwan Ram averred: "Sadhu Ram, the most fetching quality in you is your simplicity, your innocence. Your heart and mind are bereft of any human frailty, misdemeanour and iniquity. But your Guruji does not possess these qualities. He is not simple. He has all the characteristic infirmities of a mortal. Therefore, I will not give him darshan."

Sadhu Ram, the simple lad, who did not know the intricacies of life, addressed his preceptor thus: "Guruji, Bhagwan says that you are not "SIMPLE." And as such He will not give darshan to you." Hearing these words, Guruji wailed like a person lost in the labyrinth of *Bhavsagar* (the sea of life). He thought that he had got everything in life, but he could not foster and nurture simplicity, an attribute, an idiosyncrasy, God liked the most. "What is dear to Bhagwan, I lack it. Certainly, I am a deficient person. Fie on me!"

When Lord Rama found Guruji remorseful and penitent for not being simple, the all-knowing Rama, omniscient, omnipotent and merciful, took pity on Guruji and manifested himself to him. There is no gainsaying the fact that God is soon pleased by simplicity.

Verily, simplicity is the art of art, the glory of expression and the sunshine of the light of God's benediction. In character, in manner, in style, in all things, the supreme excellence is simplicity. To be simple is to be great. They that know no evil, are great, virtuous and blessed. Hence blessed are those who are simple and innocent.

CHAPTER VIII

Dan Chand, the Miser

Dan Chand lived in a small village, situated in the closer proximity of Haridwar. Notwithstanding his name being Dan Chand, that is, a man who gives charity, but in action, habit and thinking, he was quite contrary to his name. His acts were different from what is implied in his name. He was as miser, as a miser could be. He never gave even a farthing in charity to anybody. In fact, he pooh-poohed the very word, nay the very idea, of charity.

The river Ganga flowed just a kilometre away from his house, but he had never gone there to have a dip in the holy waters. He had a cogent reason behind his decision. He feared that if he went to the Ganga for a bath, the swarm of pandas encircle him, and ask for money in charity. Dan Chand was against this custom. For, by habit, he was never inclined to give charity to pandas or anyone else. So, perforce owing to his habit and thinking, he would have his daily bath at the municipal tap at his house.

There is no gainsaying the fact that there are people who possess enough money, but they do not have the "big heart" to be munificent. And Dan Chand was one such person, indeed a species of his own kind. His wife, a religious woman, repeatedly advised him to be a little charitable. She propounded that giving a small amount in charity would not make any dent in his coffers filled with wealth. She invariably reminded him that he was getting old, and before the final call of Yamraj (God of death) came, he must do some acts of bounty and exhibit magnanimity. She averred that only good deeds, qua noble karmas, stand in good stead in the next world. But Dan Chand, being Dan Chand, invariably turned a deaf ear to his wife's pleadings.

One day, it so happened that there was no water supply. The taps ran dry. Dan Chand could not take his morning bath, nor could perform the daily oblations. His wife proposed: "Why don't you go to the Ganga, and have a bath there? Nobody knows when the civic body will restore the water supply. I am told that the main water line has been damaged, and the Municipal Committee officials are making all-out efforts to repair it." But Dan Chand paid no heed to his wife's words. He, however, felt that the water supply would be restored soon enough. But the water supply could not be restored the whole day. Even the next day, too, there was no water. Dan Chand's wife reiterated his earlier suggestion that he should go to the Ganga, and have his bath. Left with no alternative, willy-nilly, he decided to go to the holy river for a bath.

The river Ganga was a little distance away. So niggardly was Dan Chand that in order to save a few farthings, he walked all the distance on foot, instead of taking a rickshaw. When he reached the Ganga ghat, he saw a crowd of people rolling and frolicking in the holy waters, and pandas waiting at the edges for *jajmans* (followers, hosts) to come out for after-bath pooja. When Dan Chand saw the pandas, he got shivers down his spine that if he bathed at the Ganga ghat, he would have to confront the pandas, who would demand money in charity. For there was, and still is, the custom at the ghats, be it Haridwar, or Varanasi that the pilgrims after the bath, donate money in charity to the priests. But Dan Chand was penny-wise. For him "charity begins at home, and ends where it begins."

Seeing the swarm of pandas, Dan Chand decided to go to the *Murda ghat* (where the rites of the dead are performed). He presumed that there would be no panda at the *Murda ghat*, and he would have a bath without being plagued and bothered by priests. He would thus escape being harried for charity.

But God willed otherwise. As soon as Dan Chand emerged out of the water after a dip, he was accosted by a panda. The emergence of a panda, all of a sudden, surprised and flabbergasted Dan Chand, a miser of misers. In fact, God too was surprised, for he had never seen a stingy person like Dan Chand. Throughout his two-score years of life, he had never come to the Ganga for fear of shelling out money in the name of charity to the priests. But today he was compelled by circumstances, partly goaded by his wife, and partly because of the stoppage of water supply at home by the civic body. But despite his coming to the Ganga ghat, not willingly but under compelling and coercive circumstances, he went to the *Murda ghat*, because he thought that there he would not be confronted by pandas. But things turned to the contrary. There too appeared a panda to pester him.

As soon as he came out of the water in a loin cloth, the panda, clad in dhoti-kurta, approached him: "*Jajman* ki jai ho!" "You have come here too," said Dan Chand. "I thought that there would be no panda at the Murda Ghat, and so I came here for a bath." The Panda replied: "Since I am a Santoshi brahmin, I prefer lonely and secluded place. I do not go to the ghat where there is a horde of pandas. Once in a while, occasionally, some *jajman* like you comes to this Murda ghat. And he gives me so much *dan* (charity) that stands in good stead for a long time. I am sure you would also give me enough money in charity to sustain me for months." Hearing the words of the panda, and his expectation from him, Dan Chand trembled in his loin cloth. In his garrulous voice, he averred: "Since I don't believe in charity, I will not give you even a penny." But the panda, who was actually the Supreme Lord in disguise, spoke in a condescending and conciliatory tone: "Charity symbolises dharma. If you give money in charity here in this earthly world, you will have treasure in the heaven. For God loves a cheerful giver. He gives twice to the one who gives promptly. It is a kind of respect, nay honour, which God bestows on the alms giver. Nevertheless, if you cannot give me that much money which may help me keep the wolf away from the door for a long time, you can give me money that may last for a couple of weeks." But these didactic dictums had no salubrious effect on Dan Chand. He said: "No! Don't trouble me. Leave me alone. I would not give you even a *dhela* (farthing)." The Panda reiterated: "If you cannot give money that may sustain me for two weeks, then let it be for a week." Dan Chand finally said: "Not even for a day." However, the panda insisted that unless you give some money in in charity, I will not let you go." Dan Chand, in order to get out of the pestering predicament, told the Panda: "I do not have any money with me at the moment. *Udhar kar lo.* For the time being, let it be deemed as a loan. I remain under your debt."

As aforementioned the Panda was none other than Lord Vishnu disguised as a panda. The Panda agreed to the proposal for a deferred payment. So, Lord Vishnu took a promise of payment of one *dhela* (penny or farthing) later on demand. The deal made Dan Chand happy. He presumed that the panda was not likely to call on him for a *dhela* (penny). But Dan Chand was "penny wise and penny foolish." For he did not expect that the Panda would ever call on him at his house, and harry him for a farthing. So, from the Ganga ghat, he returned home on foot.

When he returned home, it was almost late evening. Happy and relieved as he felt that he got rid of the panda, he went to sleep and had a sound sleep as if he had never had such a deep sleep before. In the morning next day, there was a knocking at the door. Sarla, Dan Chand's wife, opened the door. She saw a man dressed in a white dhoti-kurta, looking like a priest, standing at the door. On enquiry, the panda told the housewife: "I am a panda. I have come to take a *dhela* Dan Chand had promised to pay on account of charity." Sarla rushed in, woke up her husband, and told him that at the gate was standing a priest and that he had come to collect the charity as promised by him. Dan Chand told her to send the Panda away by telling him that her husband was not well, and that he was confined to the bed, and that he should come on some other day to collect the promised charity.

Just then the priest showed his concern for the ailing Dan Chand. He intervened: "Your husband is my *jajman.* If he is sick, it is my duty to look after him, and care and caress him in his ailment. At this juncture whether I get the promised charity or not, it hardly matters." So, the panda barged into the house and straight away went to the room where Dan Chand was lying supine on the bed. He touched his head affectionately, and said: "I would stay in the house till Dan Chand is restored to health." He requested Sarla to make arrangements for his food and stay: "I will prepare the prasad here, and offer a part of it to Dan Chand." When Dan Chand saw the panda, he was surprised and baffled.

Dan Chand felt aghast. He decided not to pay even a farthing he had promised in charity. He then devised a strategy. He was a practising yogi. He did pranayama every day. He could withhold his breath for a very long time. Accordingly, he withheld his breath and asked his wife to tell the Panda that Dan Chand had breathed his last. Sarla did what her husband asked her to do. On hearing that Dan Chand was no more, the panda felt sorry. He said: "Devi! In this hour of grief, it is enjoined on me to join the family and make all arrangements for the cremation of the deceased. So, he went around the village and informed every denizen that Dan Chand had died. He said: "Ram! Ram! Ram! My *jajman* has passed away. I urge upon all the residents of the village to join the cremation rites of the departed soul." Soon the villagers gathered there in a large number. The panda pleaded that since he was the family priest, he must accompany the dead body and help its cremation at the Murda ghat.

The rural folk that gathered to participate in the cremation rites of the presumed death of Dan Chand, consoled Sarla: "Devi! One who is born, has to die. Who can escape death? Dan Chand was still in his forties. That was not the age for him to die. But none has the power to withstand the prowess of Yamraj. So, sister, put up with what is a fate accompli. Don't lose heart. Fulfil your filial duties." However, Sarla wailed loudly and looked morose. But Dan Chand was a queer, mystifying person. He saw his wife crying, and the people of the village gathered there in a large number. But the obtained scenario had no effect on him. Eventually, the villagers made preparations to take the dead body to the Murda ghat. There they collected the wooden logs, prepared the *chita* (funeral pyre), and laid the dead body on it for burning. Yet Dan Chand was still unperturbed; he continued to hold back his breath. The Panda, qua God, thought that He had never seen such an obstinate and intractable person. He died without dying. "He is alive, and yet he has adopted the subterfuge, the ploy, of death." Dan Chand was, at last, put on the pyre. The villagers were ready to ignite the fire. Just then the panda, qua God said: "Please wait for a while. He was my *jajman*. I want to whisper some mantra in his ears so that his soul goes to the heaven." The panda whispered in the ears of Dan Chand: "I am no panda. I am Lord Vishnu. I have come to take you to *Baikunth* (Heaven), where you will be free from all worries and wants."

When Dan Chand heard that the panda was, in fact, the incarnation of Lord Vishnu, he opened his eyes promptly. He was startled and amazed that the same panda was standing before him. He closed his eyes again. The Supreme Lord reiterated: "I am really Lord Vishnu. I stand vanquished by your mulish obstinacy, your stubborn disposition. I will not take anything from you. Please ask for any boon. I shall fulfil your wish." Dan Chand spoke in a hush-hush voice: "Lord! release me from the debt of *dhela* (farthing) that I owe you. Discharge me from the debt. My only wish is that you don't ask for any charity." Lord Vishnu smiled and allowed Dan Chand's soul to fly to the next world to have a locus in Heaven.

CHAPTER IX

Man Proposes, God Disposes

There lived a Sadhu in a small town. He had his cottage outside the habitation. He sustained himself on alms. Every day he woke up in the wee hours, did oblations, and performed puja in a temple adjoining his hut. After completing his morning routine, accoutered in saffron clothes with a club in his hand and a begging bowl, he would go around the sparsely populated areas to beg alms. He never desired plenty. When he got alms sufficient to sustain himself for a day, he would return home. Throughout the day he would utter prayers, chant mantras, and engrossed himself in God's worship. He was a staunch devotee of Lord Shiva.

One day, a little after sunrise, he came to the town to beg alms as per his daily routine. He knocked at the doors of some denizens, shouting: "*Bhikshan Dehi.*" (give me alms). The previous night it had rained cats and dogs, which made the weather chilly. He felt the impact of the cold wave coming from the Himalayas. On such a cold day a sweet seller had opened his shop a little earlier than his routine, thinking that since the weather was chilly, people would throng his shop for a glass of hot milk which was boiling in one pan, and some hot *jalabies* (a sweet) which he was roasting in oil in another pan. The mendicant, lured by the sweet smell of hot *Jalabies* and the boiling milk, tarried a little in front of the sweet shop. He stood quietly in front of the hearth to warm himself. Neither the Sadhu said anything, nor the sweet seller, notwithstanding the fact that the hermit was feeling uneasy owing to hunger. The Sadhu wanted to eat *Jalabies*, but did not have money in his pocket. However, after standing before the hearth for a while, he decided to go. As soon as he turned his back, and moved his steps forward to go to some other house to ask for food, suddenly the *Halwai* (sweet seller) called him and beckoned him to come. He gave the hermit some *Jalabies* on a plate and a mug of hot milk.

The hermit ate *Jalabies* and drank hot milk with relish. His hunger was slaked. The hermit then lifted his hands above his head and profusely blessed the sweet seller. His unique gesture indicated that he was supplicating to Lord Shiva to bless the pious-hearted *Halwai.* The mendicant then picked up his stick and the begging bowl and marched ahead. The Sadhu's belly was now full with the rich breakfast.

Unaware of the vicissitudes and affliction of the common populace, Sadhu Baba engrossed in his own salubrious thoughts, sauntered slowly through the muddy water that had collected on the road. The chappal that he was wearing made the muddy water rebound all around. He did not know that a newly married young couple, newly married, was trudging behind. The couple was trying its best to avoid the dirty water. The Sadhu was walking in his joyous mood enlivened by exhilaration. In his ecstasy, he tapped his feet in the dirty water. The water sprang up and besmirched with mud the clothes of the young lady. Her young husband could not tolerate this incivility and absurdity. The lady's costly dress being spoiled with slush impelled her husband to lose the cool of his mind. He was literally in wrath, because he loved his wife dearly, and as such was unwilling to ignore the misdemeanor of the hermit. He rolled up his sleeves, caught hold of the Sadhu and dragged him in the mud. Then he said: "You fool! Are you blind? Can't you see that because of your folly and indiscretion the clothes of my wife have been dirtied? The holy man stood there flabbergasted like a pole. He was ruminating over the incident. The silence of the Sadhu further infuriated the young man. The woman lurched forward and tried to persuade her husband, red with anger, to let the holy man go. But she failed to disengage her husband. The young man would not release the Sadhu from his clutches. The intervention of his wife rather augmented his rage. Seeing her husband in a waspish mood, she stepped aside, lest he should hit her. The pedestrians on the road saw the quarrelsome young man abusing and dragging the hermit. They collected there but showed no penchant to prevail upon the irascible young man not to precipitate the matter. In fact, the common people seeing the young man incensed and exasperated, afeared him. They stepped aside and stood at a distance. As the ire of the young man accentuated into fury, he slapped the mendicant. All of a sudden, the Sadhu uttered; "Wah God! Just a little while ago, the magnanimous poor sweet-seller slaked my hunger with milk and *Jalabies*, and now I got a hot slap on my cheeks. Verily, strange are your ways my Lord Shiva. Nevertheless, I have no complaint. For whatever God does is right. God is always benevolent to his devotees." Uttering these words, the hermit rubbed his cheeks and ambled forward chanting some mantra to knock at some other door for alms.

On the other hand, the young pair dallying in amorous mood, laughing and giggling, oblivious of the rancorous mishap that happened a little while ago, reached the door of their house. The young man took the keys out of his pocket, and hurriedly climbed up the stairs to open the door. Owing to the heavy rains, the marble-stairs had become slippery. All of a sudden, the young man slipped on the stairs, and came tumbling down. The woman shrieked, cried and wept, attracting the attention of the street-walkers and sought their assistance. Soon a huge crowd collected there. They lifted the "fallen" young man. But it was too late. The young man had suffered a fatal head injury, and because of the excessive bleeding, he died on the spot.

Some people had seen the Sadhu Baba coming to the spot post-haste. Seeing the mendicant, they began to whisper that since the hermit was slapped by the young man, he cursed him. Obviously, it is as a result of the curse that the man in the prime of his youth had died. Otherwise, how could a young man die just by slipping from the stairs? Some mischievous people in the crowd believed the story of the curse. They encircled the Sadhu. One of them said: "What kind of devotee of God are you? Owing to just one slap, you have cursed the young man and taken his life. The holy men, devotees of God, are free from anger and retaliation. Instead of putting up with a little trouble, you lost the sense of tolerance and cursed the young man."

But the Sadhu Baba, innocent as he was, replied; "By Lord Shiva, I have not cursed this young man." But the crowd in unison asked: "If you have not cursed the young man, then how did he die after falling from the stairs?" Then the hermit asked the crowd a simple question. "Is there anybody amongst you who is an eye-witness to this mishap?" Out of the crowd came forward a middle-aged person, who said: "Yes! I am the eyewitness of this incident." Then the hermit asked: "Did the mud that sprang owing to my feet, spoil the clothes of the young man?" The man replied: "No. But the woman's dress was spoiled." The mendicant then held the questioner from his arms, and asked: "Then why did the young man beat me up?" The questioner then pointed out: "Since the young man was the lover of the woman, he could not tolerate her clothes being sullied. That is why he slapped you."

Hearing the reply of a common man in the crowd, the hermit laughed and averred: "By God I have never cursed anybody. But there is "Somebody", you may call Him by any name, God, Lod Shiva, Lord Vishnu, who loves me. If the lover/friend of the woman could not stomach the "hurt" meted out to his beloved, then how could "my Friend, my Lover" tolerate if someone thrashes his dear devotee, his lover. Even the biggest of all men, be he a king, or any other parson of high rank, must remember that God will batter him, cudgel him, if he causes any harm to his devotee qua friend, or lover. It is true that the 'lathi' of God is not seen, but when it hits/ lashes, it causes great pain. Our good action saves us from God's lathi (club). For actions speak louder than words. For a generous action is its own reward. All breathing human beings must realize the truth instinctively that all the noble sentiments in the world weigh less than a single lovely action. The young man did not listen to the good counsel of his dear wife. Had he followed her advice, he must have escaped the calamity. The old adage that "man proposes, and God disposes," is true to every syllable. Uttering these sane words, the mendicant embarked on his daily routine to knock at the doors of other men, giving a call: *Bhikshan Dehi.*

CHAPTER X

Wealth Cannot Buy Time

Mani Ram, aged 50, lived in a small town. He had a big business of import and export. Greed had been the sine qua non of his life. The main aim, nay the only aim, of his life, was to expand his business and collect as much wealth as possible. He was the true personification of the old adage, "penny wise pound foolish." Though he had plenty of lucre, he was, by habit and nature, niggardly; he was acquisitive and close-fisted, and had never spent money, either on himself or on his wife and children. He never indulged in any kind of entertainment, such as going to the theatre, visiting places of tourist interest, or even defraying money on clothes. He never did any act of philanthropy and altruism, for such acts entailed expenditure. He believed that all the beautiful sentiments in the world were not worth spending money. He was true to his name--Mani Ram-- for "money" was his "Ram;" his God.

His wife, named Savitri, who was a paragon of virtues, was unlike her husband. She was a devotee of Lord Krishna. She was a good-natured and a humane human being. One day, after dusk, she and her husband, sat on the bed together. It was the winter season, the days were shorter, and the nights fell earlier. Before going to bed, Savitri reminded Mani Ram, her husband, that earning and earning money and gathering wealth, should not be made the be-all and end-all of life. She opined that money was like a muck not worth collecting. She further said that money was like manure: "If you pile it up in one place, it stinks like hell. But if you spread it around, it does a lot of good. Money never goes with the moneyed man, for there is no pocket in a shroud."

But Mani Ram pooh-poohed her ideas. He negated her philosophy as just an empty discourse. In his opinion "wealth is the best recipe for happiness." He advised his wife: "Savitri! If you want to know what God thinks of money, you have only to look at those who are affluent and blessed with plenty and abundance. Wealth makes many friends, whereas poverty is shunned by everybody." However, the prolonged powwow on the subject of "good" and "bad" wealth, made Mani Ram drowsy and he went to sleep.

In the sleep, Mani Ram had a horrible dream. Even in his deep sleep, it was again the subject of wealth that was further accentuated. He felt that he had died and that Yamraj, the god of Death, himself descended to the earth to take him away to the other world. He ruminated that he might have done some good in his life that the god of Death himself came to escort him to the heaven. What surprised him further was something unusual. As soon as he reached the heaven, Lord Indra, the Chief of gods, came out of his heavenly abode, and took him to the celestial apartments. Mani Ram was told to stay there. Then Indra saw a bag in Mani Ram's hands. He enquired: "What is in this bag you have carried all the way from the world of mortals to the world of immortals?" Mani Ram replied: "This is a bag very close to my heart, for it contains crores of rupees which I earned on the earth through my lucrative avocation." Indra said: "Ok! Keep your bag in locker number 'nine,' situated in the left-hand corner of the apartment allotted to you." The Chief of gods indicated with his forefinger towards the deposit vault. Mani Ram, as advised and directed, put his bag of money in the locker. He locked it and kept the key with himself. He was pleased to see the room allotted to him, which was well-furnished, comfortable, soothing, spic and span.

After settling down in the room allotted to him, Mani Ram thought of having a look at the celestial market of the *Indraloka* (the abode of Lord Indra and other gods). While sauntering through the neat and clean roads and alleys, bustling with well-accoutered apsaras (celestial dancers) and heavenly denizens, he eventually reached a huge shopping mall. There were strange things, unseen before, stocked there. The earthly trader was lured by them. He scanned through the shopping mall, selected some items, and put them into a basket, the way people do on the earth. Then he went to the counter to make the payment for the articles he had selected to buy. He took out a couple of 500-rupee new notes, and gave them to the damsel at the counter. But she refused to accept the earthly currency: "Sir! This currency is alien to *Indraloka*, and as such it is not accepted here. It may be a legal tender on the earth, but not here." Hearing this, Mani Ram's face fell down. He felt as if several poisonous snakes hissed around his head. His legs shook. He staggered. He was flabbergasted and confounded. and could not believe that the money earned by him so laboriously and covetously, could not buy anything in the other world, qua the world of *Indraloka*. He felt peeved and thought of making a complaint. Mani Ram then approached Lord Indra and complained to him against the apsara-like damsel sitting at the counter that she refused to accept the cash offered to her as payment for the goods purchased. The only reaction Lord Indra exhibited, was a smile. He told Mani Ram that notwithstanding his being a businessman, and an experienced trader, he was unschooled and uninformed that the currency of one country was not accepted by any other country. "For instance, the currency of Japan is not accepted in Russia, or that of Sri Lanka is not accepted in India, and vice-versa. Therefore, the currency of the earth is not the legal tender in the heaven. It was an act of inanity, of stupidity, on your part, to use the earthly currency here. Your rigmarole has surprised me."

Hearing the words of Indra, Mani Ram lost his mental ingenuity that all that he had earned on the earth, had gone waste, and became useless. He started crying loudly, puling and puking: "Oh God! What has happened? I am completely ruined. I worked hard day and night, to earn money. I was so much preoccupied with gathering wealth that I did not spend even a penny on myself, nor on my family, wife and children, nor even on my aged parents. I did no charitable act, no act of munificence, of philanthropy. For me, money spoke, money reigned, money did everything. I did not find time even to meet my friend, my kith and kin, my well-wishers. Throughout my life, I did not take a rest, and enjoyed no entertainment. I was always greedy for filthy lucre; I had become avarice personified. And now all that money is of no use; it has become a heap of muck." Mani Ram realized, though belatedly, that the love for money was the mother of all evil. He felt that what he did, was true to the old maxim: "penny wise pound foolish." Verily, when money speaks, truth becomes silent.

Lord Indra showed the right type of reaction expected of a god. He pointed out: "Mani Ram, your lament is futile; you will not get anything; it is like crying over spilled milk. The money deposited in the lockers of the Heaven, by many a big businessman, like Jamshedji Tata, Dhirubhai Ambani, etc., has perished. So much so that even the American Dollar or British Pound have no worth here. The currency that works in heaven is of a different denomination."

Mani Ram finally asked: "Lord Indra! Kindly tell me which is that currency, that legal tender, which has the appreciative and acceptable value here?" Indra replied that the "currency which is accepted here is different from that of the earth. That currency includes noble action, which a mortal human being does on the earth. What is regularly deposited into the account of a mortal includes the service a man renders to those who are in distress, befriends a man afflicted with grief, penury, and ailment; makes a moaning person laugh; gleefully arranges the marriage of a girl belonging to a poor family; provides education to poor kids and make them capable human beings; helping those addicted to drugs or other vices and cure them of that vice; supporting with money a school, a temple, or an Old Age Home. Such persons, engrossed in charitable and philanthropic acts, have credit in *Indraloka*. They are provided with "Credit Cards," which when they come to this world, can use in heaven and live in bliss here. Sweet words, and good behavior, make a human being great. Money can make a man rich; but the real wealthy person is the one who has noble mind, noble thinking, and noble friends."

Good deeds, qua righteousness actions, respect for all human beings, and exhibiting sentiments of mercy and pity, are the credit-worthy virtues which account for a Credit Card in the Heaven. For mercy has a human heart, pity a human face, and love is the human form divine. If a man wants to be respected, let him go and sell that which he has and give it to the poor; such a man shall have treasure in heaven.

Mani Ram fell at the feet of Lord Indra: "Lord! I know I am a sinner. But with your blessings, I can be rid of all the dross and transformed into purity." Lord Indra said; "*Tathastu,* Be it so." Then Mani Ram suddenly woke up into the waking world.

Dreams may or may not be true, but there is no gainsaying the fact that a niggardly person, an avaricious opulence personified, at long last comes to grief. His wealth comes to naught. After death, he can't take even a farthing with him; he leaves behind all that he has.

Soon after what Mani Ram saw in his dream, something untoward happened. One day *yamdoot* (the messenger of the god of Death) came to him and said that his time was up. The trader implored that all his life he had only worked to garner wealth and that he could not get time to make use of it. He requested the messengers of Death to grant him an extension in life to enable him to make proper use of his huge wealth. All through his life he did not spend even a penny on himself and his family to enjoy life. But the *Yamdoots* refused to grant his supplication, and repeated that his "time is up." Mani Ram repeated his entreaty that if he was given a year's time, he would give one million gold coins to them in exchange for the extension in life. But the messengers of Death repelled his offer. However, the wealthy trader, could not be deterred. He knew the ways of the world, especially the ways of the world of business and trade. This time he made a bigger offer of two million gold coins if he was allowed a time of six months to live. But *Yamdoots* again refused his request; for it was not in their powers to extend the span of his life. Then Mani Ram implored for the extension of one month, and when the same was refused, he reiterated his request for a day's time. But all in vain. The messengers of Death refused to relent, despite being lured with more and more lucrative offers. Finally, he supplicated that he would give them all his wealth if the *yamdoots* allowed him a very short time of one hour. The *Yamdoots* asked him as to what would he do with one hour. Mani Ram said: "I need a little time to reflect and write my will, I need time to divide my wealth among my kith and kin, and apportion a part of it to my servants and minions, as also to the poor and the needy, I never remembered and cared for, as I remained possessive and covetous in my life." The messengers of Death said that for that purpose just ten minutes would be enough. So, Mani Ram was given an extension of ten minutes. Obviously, money can buy the denizens of the mortal world, but not of the world beyond this world.

Finally, Mani Ram, with tears of repentance and remorse, in his eyes, wrote: "Among the jingle of gold coins, I turned a deaf ear to the value of time. Wealth may buy anything and everything, but it cannot buy time." And with this, Death's messengers took him away.

Down the ages, our sages have given us sound advice, but with the passage of time, we became oblivious of what we were taught. One day Guru Nanak Dev Ji, during his travelling, reached Lahore. He called Duni Chand, a Revenue Officer, who had amassed dirty lucre through immoral and unrighteous means. The Guru Great gave him a needle and told him that this would bring him more luck, but he should return the needle to him after his death. Duni Chand thought for a moment and then said that after death, when he ceased to be living, how would he return the needle. Then Guru Nanak said: "If you cannot take the needle with you after death, how can you take all the wealth you have amassed with you to the other world." Duni Chand had a self-realization, and soon after mended his ways, and became a devoted disciple of Guru Nanak.

There is no gainsaying the fact that "now is the accepted time. Time management in time is the key to success." Everyone has a rendezvous with death. And with death die all our plans, hopes, aspirations and expectations. Yet people do not value time, and formulate all kinds of stratagems to amass power and pelf. Truly, wealth accumulates, but man decays. Verily, there is enough for everyone's needs, but not enough for everyone's greed.

CHAPTER XI

Tale of an Honest School Master

One day a school teacher was returning home. On the way, there was a rivulet. He tried to cross it. But his mood changed. The ambience was salubrious. The wind was pleasant, soothing and balsamic. A banyan tree with thick foliage grew on the bank of the stream. The teacher decided to sit there under the shade of a tree on a stone slab. He opened his bag, took out a pen, and started writing about the arithmetic of his salary on a piece of paper. Suddenly, the pen fell into the torrential brook; only the cap of the pen remained in his hands.

The happening caused a lot of woe and anguish to the teacher, for he had purchased that pen from the market a day before. He made all-out efforts to search for the pen. He got down into the water in search of the pen. Afeared lest he should be drowned into the surging currents of the rill, willy-nilly he came out. Since it was a new pen, the teacher was not willing to abandon the search. He sat under the tree and supplicated to God to help him find the pen. Just then there rose a huge wave in the water, and out of it emerged Varun, the god of water.

The Teacher got surprised and flabbergasted. He recalled the story of the woodcutter who had lost his axe, and how the demigod of water helped him recover his axe. Nevertheless, the deity emanating out of the brook asked: "Guruji, why are you so perturbed? What can I do for you? Do you want promotion, or transfer to some more lucrative place, or increment?" The teacher felt enthused by the offer. He asked: "Who are you? And why do you want to help me?" The demigod said: "I am Varun, the god of water." On hearing this, the teacher promptly demanded: "Sire! I had purchased a pen yesterday morning. Look at this cap of the pen. Just a little while ago, the pen fell into the water of the rivulet, while I was writing about the account of my salary. You can help me find the pen." Varun asked: "Are you sad for only this minor problem? Let me take a dip in the water, and bring the pen for you." Varun dived into the water, and emerged with a shining pen made of silver. "Here is your pen," said Varun. "No sir! This is not my pen. I am a poor teacher. I cannot afford a costly pen made of silver." Varun averred: "Don't worry. Let me dive for the second time in search of your pen." God of water, this time, brought a pen made of gold. "Guruji, take this pen. It must be yours," said Varun. However, the teacher requested: "Such a costly pen, and that too mine! Sire, you are joking and making fun of me. I am just an ordinary teacher of a school in the village. How can I have such an expensive pen?"

Varun assured the teacher that he should not bother, nor he should have any apprehension. He said that he would dive into the steam for one more time, his last dip, and come out with the right pen. This time god of water brought out the original pen of the school teacher. The teacher jumped and danced in glee, and shouted vociferously: "Yes! This is my pen." Varun, pleased with his honesty, pointed out: "Guruji, you have won my heart. Therefore, keep all the three pens."

Guruji came home. He narrated the entire story to his wife and showed the glittering costly pens to her. She did not believe the narration of her husband; "you might have stolen these pens from some shop or house." The teacher did not like the way his wife doubted his integrity and blamed him of thieving and falsehood. He did his best to convince her of his scrupulous and righteous character, but to no avail. Left with no alternative, he took his sceptical wife to the scene of the occurrence. Both sat under the banyan tree on the stone slab. The teacher explained in detail, bit by bit, all that happened. She was connecting all the loose ends of the story like a police officer, when suddenly she slipped into the brook. Guruji was confused and sad. He started lamenting loudly, when suddenly the waves rose, piercing through the ripples, Varun emerged once again. "Now what has happened? Why are crying again?" Guruji narrated the story as to what had happened. "Don't weep! Have courage and patience. I will bring your wife out just now," said Varun.

The god of water dived into the water and came out with a beautiful woman, a prototype of Madhuri Dixit. Varun asked: "Is this your wife?" The teacher said: "Yes! This is my wife." Now it was the turn of Varun: "Scoundrel. You are lying. I will now punish you, and teach you a lesson." Varun was about to curse him, when the teacher fell at the feet of the demigod, and solicited his mercy. "Please forgive me. I have committed no wrong. If I had said no, you would have dipped into the water again, and brought out a duplicate of Katrina Kaif. Even then if I had said no, you would have dived into the water again, and brought out my wife, and then given all the three 'lasses' to me. How could I afford three women being a poor teacher? Varuna smiled, brought out his wife, and went away.

CHAPTER XII

The Camel Tale and the two Gems

There lived a rich merchant in a certain town, where was held an animal fair at regular intervals for selling and buying animals, camels, horses, donkeys, bulls, etc. One day, the said merchant, named Sadhu Ram, on a casual jaunt, per chance reached the fair site. There he espied a camel, young and sturdy. He thought of buying it. He negotiated the deal with the owner of the camel and bought the animal. As soon as Sadhu Ram reached home with the animal in tow, he summoned Sudhir, his servant, and directed him to remove the saddle, so that the animal could relax and graze in the fields close by. When the servant removed the saddle from the hunch-back of the camel, he found underneath a small velvet pouch. When he opened it, he was surprised to find that the pouch contained precious gems in it. In his excitement and eagerness, he shouted: "Master, you have purchased a camel. But under the saddle, there is a pouch full of diamonds, which, it seems, you have got gratis. Obviously, with the animal, the seller has given you gems as a free gift."

When the merchant heard this, he came running. He was, literally amazed and startled to see the jewels, radiating and gleaming in the glimmer of the sun. Sadhu Ram, the merchant, remarked: "I have purchased a camel and not the jewels. I must rush back to the fair market and return the treasure to the seller, a rural denizen." But Sudhir, his servant, thought differently. He felt that his master might be a dunce, a block-head. He proposed: "Sir! Keep the jewels. Nobody would have an inkling about it; nobody would even know about the treasure, you have found by chance. It is the handiwork of dame luck." But Sadhu Ram turned a deaf ear to the suggestion of his servant. He rushed back to the fair site post-haste, located the owner of the camel, and returned the pouch to him. This gesture of honesty pleased the camel-seller. He said: "I had forgotten that I had hidden the costly gem-stones underneath the saddle. I want to reward you for your integrity and uprightness. You can pick any two diamonds from the lot." But Sadhu Ram, being, literally a man having idiosyncrasies of a sadhu, of a sage, refused. He averred: "I have paid the right price for the animal. Therefore, I do not need any pecuniary recompense, as a gift of gratitude from you." But the camel seller insisted on gratifying the act of honesty of Sadhu Ram. When pressed too much, the merchant at long last, said: "When I opened the pouch and saw sparkling gems, I stole two priceless pieces and pocketed them."

After this unexpected admission, qua confession, the farmer lost the cool of his mind. He immediately started counting the gems as to which were the pieces that the merchant pilfered. He emptied the pouch and counted the jewels one by one. To his utter surprise, the farmer found that all the jewels were there, and no gem was missing. To be doubly sure, he counted the gems once again and found that his treasure was intact sans any loss. He was confounded a great deal, for he did not know as to which were the two diamonds which the merchant said to have pilfered.

Seeing the discomfiture of the farmer, Sadhu Ram announced: "The two gems I Have stolen, are my integrity and self-respect." He propounded, "We have to look within to find whether we have these two jewels (integrity and self-esteem). Those who have these two invaluable, highly precious gems of pure ray serene, they are the richest human beings in the world."

CHAPTER XIII

Goodness Begets Goodness

Krishan Murari, after completing his medical education, opened a clinic in his hometown. Soon reports of his professional acumen spread in the nearby rural areas. Patients thronged to him for treatment of all kinds of ailments. With the passage of time, he became so renowned that he opened a small hospital. He ran it proficiently with the assistance of competent medicos and well-trained paramedical staff.

One day something unexpected happened. In his hospital was brought a patient, named Ashish. He was suffering from high fever, dry cough and respiratory stress. His condition was serious. Dr Krishan Murari examined him thoroughly and admitted him in the ICU. The doctor told his staff to provide him with the best medical care. He also ordered that the patient should not be charged for medicines and treatment, or for any other hospital expenses. Within days Ashish was fully recovered. The Hospital discharged him. A medical bill of over two lakhs was placed before doctor Krishan Murari. The doctor summoned his Accounts Manager and told him not to charge any money from the patient, and directed him to bring the patient to his room.

Ashish was brought on a wheelchair to doctor Krishan Murari's chamber. Then the doctor asked Ashish: "Bhai, do you recognise me?" Ashish said: "It appears I have seen you earlier somewhere, but I do not recall exactly where and in what circumstances." The doctor nudged and stimulated Ashish's memory: "Remember your chance meeting me at a lonely place about two years ago? It was the time of sunset, and there was dense forest all around. And in that savage wilderness, you had repaired my car." Then the doctor narrated the whole incident as to what happened on that day when he was stranded with his wife and two kids at a lonely place in the midst of a thick forest. "On that fateful day, I had gone to visit the famous Krishna temple, situated at a distance of about seventy kilometres from my house. I took my car in the morning and embarked on the holy pilgrimage. On the way, we had lunch at a wayside dhaba. Eventually, we reached the holy shrine in the afternoon and paid our obeisance to Lord Krishna. Late in the evening, we began our return journey. Soon it was twilight. As ill luck would have it, my car stopped. I tried to restart it, but could not. In the semi-darkness of the fast-spreading dusk, I felt marooned and deserted in the jungle. There was no expectation of any motor-mechanic who would emerge from somewhere to repair the fault and start the car. My wife and kids afeared the unforeseen fear lurking in the forest. The very thought of spending the night in the deep forest at a lonely place with all kinds of ferocious animals prowling in the nocturnal gloom, unnerved us. We were, literally praying to God to send some help to take us out of this difficult plight. Feeling uneasy, when we were ruminating over the uncanny predicament, just then within moments, there happened something in a flash. Our faces gleamed. We saw a young man coming on a scooter. I raised my hand in a gesture to stop you. And you were kind enough to pull up your vehicle. Verily, we felt that God had sent you to help us."

The doctor further added: "Ashish (now I know your name), you were good enough to get down from your scooter, and enquired: "What the matter is? And why are you standing in the middle of the road with your wife and children and that too in the wild at such a time of the night?" When you heard our tale of woe, you opened the bonnet of the car, looked inside, and set the fault right. The car started. Later, you told me that you ran a garage. I felt highly grateful to you for rendering this yeoman's service."

Krishan Murari said "notwithstanding having enough money, I could not get any help in such a strenuous and onerous morass. In such an arduous state, you helped us get out of the predicament. This kind of timely aid is invaluable; it cannot be determined in terms of money. However, when I humbly asked you as to how much money I should pay to you on account of my gratitude, you refused to accept any pecuniary reward. What you said at that time, the words you spoke, turned out to be my inspiration for the rest of my life." At that trying moment you had said: "It is the principle of my life not to charge any money from a person in trouble, in distress. For I staunchly believe in the tenet that it is God who keeps account of the labour, which a man puts in to help a fellow human being in need."

The doctor averred that "On that day I was highly impressed by what you said. I felt that when an ordinary person can follow such high ethics in life, why can't I do the same thing? So, I had resolved that I would provide free medical service and treatment to poor patients, and those having meagre income. I had made up my mind for aye."

It has been more than two years that the kind doctor had been acting on this humane canon; it became a conceptual ideal for him. Krishan Marari told Ashish: "Since then I have not felt any dearth of money; rather I am earning much more than I earned before." The doctor assured Ashish: "This hospital is mine. You are my guest here. I conform to your dictum and stick to the path of goodness you have manifested to me. And as such I would not charge any money from you. For goodness begets goodness." Krishan Murari further eulogised: "I am beholden, nay indebted, to God that He had granted me an opportunity to serve the man who provided me with a motivation to serve those needing medical care. Like you, the Almighty above will keep account of my good deed too." The doctor asked Ashish to go home without any compunction. In future too if he had any problem, he could come for help sans any hesitation.

Ashish, while leaving the room of Doctor Krishan Murari, obliged and gratified, espied a statue of Lord Krishna on the mantle in the doctor's chamber. He laid prostrate before the deity and paid his obeisance. Then he supplicated to Lord Krishna: "My Lord! Today you have acquitted my "labour," my action of goodness, my account, with proliferated interest."

Lord Krishna in the Gita postulates:
Karmanyevadhikaraste

ma phalesu kadachana
ma karmaphalaheturbhur
ma te sango stvakarmani
(Ch 2: verse 47)

Krishna tells Arjuna that he has the right to action, but not to its fruits. That is to say that when we do our work, plough or paint, sing or think, repair a car or cure a patient, it should be a desireless action, for man has right to action but not to its fruits, qua rewards. Nothing matters except the goodwill, the willing fulfilment of God's purpose. There is no gainsaying the fact that man is entitled to the performance of action, but not to its rewards thereof. One should neither desire rewards of action nor be drawn to inaction. This is the message conveyed by the aforementioned parable.

CHAPTER XIV

God's Law of Magnanimity

It happened many years ago in Calcutta, where lived a renowned Doctor Rishi Kumar. Once his aged mother fell ill. With the passage of time, her ailment worsened. There was no hope for her survival left. One day in the late evening when the nocturnal gloom was spreading fast, Rishi Babu as he was popularly called, approached her mother and affectionately asked: "Mother dear! If you have any desire for anything, please let me know. I will fulfil your wish." Rishi's mother remained quiet for a little while. Then she said: "Rishi, a couple of months ago, I had eaten *Anjeer* (fig fruit) of Bombay. I long for that fruit if you could procure it."

During those days *Anjeer* was not available in the fruit and vegetable market of Calcutta. Rishi became depressed and introspective. He ruminated that if he ordered *Anjeer* from Bombay, it would take several weeks to arrive by train from Bombay to Calcutta, for there was no air flight from Bombay to Calcutta during those days. This caused a lot of discomfiture and agony to Rishi Babu as he was not able to fulfil the last wish of his mother. He became pensive: "What an unlucky son I am that my mother's last desire could not be fulfilled by me." Willy-nilly, he was filled with self-reproach. The famous Doctor was at a loss to arrive at any tangible solution to alleviate his predicament and discharge his filial obligation to gratify his mother's last desire. Even if he contacted some friend in Bombay, to bring the fig fruit to fulfil the wish of his ailing mother, it would have taken a long time to reach Calcutta. "Till then my mother may or may not survive," he thought.

Rishi Babu went to his room and sprawled on his bed dejected and doleful. He wept bitterly: "Oh God! Am I so unfortunate that I cannot satisfy the last wish of my mother whom I love the most." It was almost midnight when he heard a knock at his door. The Doctor Babu thought that it might be some patient needing medical help.

But Rishi was in no mood to open the door, and go out and attend to and treat the patient. He shouted from inside the room: "Please come in the morning. At this time, I am not in a mood to go with you to attend the medical emergency." The man standing outside, banged the door again, this time more fiercely. Raising his garrulous voice, he said: "I am not a patient. I have come to you at the instance of my master. I have brought something for you; a packet which your friend, Kuldeep Sharma, has sent for you. So, please open the door."

Hearing the name of his friend, Rishi Babu got up from his bed immediately and opened the door. Outside was standing a messenger with a basket in his hands. He handed over the basket to the Doctor and said: "Sir, my master, Shri Kuldeep Sharma, your intimate friend, has just arrived from Bombay. He would be going to Rangoon tomorrow morning. He sent this basket full of fig fruit, which he has brought from Bombay for you. He ordered me to deliver this fruit basket to you. I am sorry to bother you at this odd hour of the night, for Kuldeep Sir directed me to deliver this basket just now since he would be leaving for Rangoon very early in the morning."

Hearing the name of *Anjeer*, Rishi Babu jumped and danced in ecstasy. For he had an unexpected and surprising moment of excitement and mirth. Tears of happiness wallowed from his eyes. His body had a feeling of excitement; it was a thrilling moment for him. Rishi Babu took the fruit basket and slowly sauntered to his mother's room. He spoke gleefully, "Mother dear, bountiful and magnanimous God has sent the fig fruit for you." This brought a ray of joy to the face of the ailing woman. Seeing his mother in a mood of exultation, smiling in jubilation, Rishi Babu felt as if the benign God had blessed him with a rare boon.

Kuldeep, the friend of Rishi Babu, was a resident of Bombay, who had landed property and farm houses both in Calcutta and Rangoon. Whenever Kuldeep came from Bombay, he invariably brought fig fruit for his friend. Look at the law of Providence. Rishi's mother, seriously ill and counting her days, wanted to eat

Anjeer. But the all-knowing munificent God had made arrangements for the desired fruit four days ago, And the fruit reached Calcutta at the right time, and not a day before, not a day late. When God intends to shower his blessing, His bounty, He nominates someone to fulfil the task. In the Mahabharata, Krishna wanted to punish evil and unrighteousness and establish the rule of righteousness. For this purpose, he uses Arjuna as his nominee to destroy the sinners and reward the virtue. God is aware of all that we do, think, and desire. When God intends to help somebody, he creates a persona to act on his behalf. Kuldeep, in this story, is one such persona.

CHAPTER XV

Smile Begets Smile

Animals do not smile. Nor do they laugh. It is a gift that God has bestowed on human beings. Therefore, we should smile as much as possible. We should laugh as much as possible. For smile begets smile. Laughter begets laughter. When we smile, the world smiles with us.

There is divinity in a smile, a charming endearment. Take for example Lord Krishna who has always been depicted with a smile, irrespective of the fact whether we see him as a pampered child or as a playful boy, or as a lover in dalliance with the cowherdesses (gopis), or as a warrior, or a politician. On the battlefield at Kurukshetra, when Arjuna, filled with remorse and pity, refuses to fight and asks questions, the first reaction that Lord Krishna manifests is a smile. It is the smile of a Guru, of a counsellor, of a friend, of a philosopher. It is a pleasant smile which eventually flows into the song celestial.

That smile endears us to everyone and can be substantiated by a famous Middle-Eastern folk tale. Mulla Nasruddin always accompanied his Sultan, because Nasruddin's ready wit and humorous repartees pleased the king. Once the caravan of the Sultan was passing through a desert. He saw a small town at a distance. He proposed: "Nasruddin, let us go to this town to see as to how many inhabitants recognize their king. Don't disclose my identity to anyone. I will go there incognito."

The Sultan stayed put his caravan outside the *abadi* (habitation) and entered the town walking on foot with Nasruddin. The king was flabbergasted to realize that no denizen of the town recognized him, nor paid any reverence. But every passerby and pedestrian smiled when he saw Mulla Nasruddin. This flustered the Sultan. Irritated, he asked Nasruddin, "How is it that everybody knows my minion in the town, while nobody recognizes the Sultan." Nasruddin replied:

"Jahanpanah, these people do not know me either." "Then why did they smile seeing you," asked the king. "Honourable Sir, they smiled because I smiled to see them. For smile begets smile."

As aforementioned, Lord Krishna, qua God, manifests His divinity in His smile. Therefore, I firmly believe that there is divinity in the smile. This belief was reinforced by a story that I recently read.

A woman visited a temple every day. One day her school-going son asked: "Mother dear! Why do you go to the temple?" She replied: "I go to the temple to meet God and offer fruits and milk to Him for lunch." This caught the imagination of the little boy. The next day, he thought of meeting God. Carrying a lunch box, fruits, and soft drinks, he reached the temple. As soon as he started climbing the stairs, he saw an old woman sitting there. The child looked at her. The woman reciprocated his 'look' with a smile. The urchin felt that perhaps the old granny was hungry. So, he gave some food to her, which she gratefully ate. Then he started climbing the stairs leading to the temple. Midway, he looked back. His angelic gaze again met that of the woman. The woman smiled again. This time it was a broader smile. The child, in his innocence, thought that the woman was still hungry. He turned back, came down the stairs, and offered the entire lunch, food, fruits, etc. to her. The woman ate the food, smiled and smiled, and again smiled. Her face reflected a sanctified aura of happiness and serenity. By an involuntary and spontaneous urge, she caressed the boy's head and patted his back.

When the child returned home, he was a personification of an undefined ecstasy, peace and tranquillity. His mother asked him: "What made him so happy and so calm and composed?" The child replied: "Mother, I had lunch with God." God appeared to me in the form of an old woman who had the most charming smile, the one I had never seen before."

Meanwhile, the poor beggar-woman, resplendent in the celestial happiness, too returned home. On enquiry, she told her son that she had shared lunch with God, who was much younger to her.

This is the power of a smile, with which we can make a stranger our kin. Therefore, in order to overcome the tensions of the humdrum of life, we should smile all the while. Verily, when we smile or laugh, we look very charming, loving and loveable.

CHAPTER XVI

The Return of the Native

"I decline to accept the end of men ... I believe that man will not only endure: he will prevail. He is immortal not because he alone among creatures has an inexhaustible voice but because he has a soul, a spirit capable of compassion and sacrifice and endurance." This dictum of William Faulkner is true to life. The innate human in man never dies. Values of life, compassion, forgiveness, love, and fellow-feelings, embedded in man's soul, may often trip and prompt a man to do evil. But the sinews of virtue, lying dormant --even in the worst of men -- can be revitalized by the words of wisdom, good company, good discourse, and goodwill. The following incident, a real one, which happened a few years ago, substantiates this fact of life.

I fondly recall that a 70-plus eminent doctor, a skin specialist of international repute, who after the partition, had settled in Delhi. He had married a British lady. He was blessed with a son who had died a decade ago. He adopted a boy from the Ashram of Mother Teresa and had bequeathed his entire property to him. He had purchased land near Ghaziabad for a herbal plantation. He had been using the herbs grown in his farmhouse in his own factory for manufacturing medicines for skin diseases. At his farmhouse, he also ran a skin institute and a charitable school where free education was imparted.

On the fateful day, he had reached his farmhouse clinic, as usual, in the morning, and started attending to his patients waiting for him. Suddenly, two young men, in their early twenties, gate-crashed into his clinic, forcibly pushed him into a Van at pistol point blind-folded him, and sped away towards some unknown destination. At night when the blindfold was removed from his eyes, he found himself in a sugarcane field.

The next morning the Doctor requested his kidnappers to buy him some medicines for his eyes and blood pressure. The kidnappers willingly obliged him. The doctor kept the cool of his mind, as he was spiritually disposed to believe that he would get what was ordained for him. For him, prayer was the voice of faith. He narrated stories from the Ramayana and the Mahabharata to his captors, interspersed with discourses on the Gita and the ancient scriptures to persuade his tormentors to follow the path of righteousness. He propounded that the truth and goodness were mighty and would ultimately prevail. Surprisingly, he always found them receptive.

As the days rolled on there was an apparent change of heart in the kidnappers. They no longer tortured and abused him. On the contrary, they became respectful to him; and even massaged his legs to relieve him of the fatigue. On the New Year Day, the doctor kept fast. His captors gave him six bananas. He returned three to them. This gesture of affection and fellow-feelings had a great impact on them. They were visibly moved and subdued. Truly, kindness begets kindness. The doctor repeatedly told the kidnappers that he did not have money to pay the ransom, since his money was invested in charitable trusts.

Meanwhile, the doctor's daily discourse on spiritualism with stories culled from the ancient scriptures, awakened the conscience of the kidnappers. There was a complete metamorphosis in their attitude to life. There is no denying the fact that there is much good even in the worst of us. What is needed is the catalytic agent to convert what is brazen into the golden one. Eventually, in the second week of January, the kidnappers decided to release him.

The weather was extremely cold. The chilly winds coming down the great Himalayas had been whipping the otherwise placid and temperate plains of north India. This has been a natural phenomenon, year after year, but the winter this time had been particularly cruel and severe for the protagonist of this story. After the dusk fell and the night's black mantle covered everything, the streets in the town virtually became curfew-bound with not a soul venturing to stir out. The only sound that penetrated the silence of the night was that of the bone-piercing cold wind cracking the whip.

On one such night, on the Delhi- Haridwar Road, the wild wind suspended its fury for a moment and watched in amusement a two-wheeler, challenging its ferocity and speeding towards Sambholi, a small dusty town, about eighty miles from Delhi, with a blind-folded aged person on pillion. The man was obviously dishevelled and unkempt with anxiety and apprehension writ large on his visage.

Just a few minutes later, the frozen sugar-cane stems watched mutely old man being dumped off the scooter unceremoniously. The numerous depressions on the fog-infested sugar-cane fields would still remember the helpless groping of a stunned man who had just taken off the blindfold constricting his vision. The fields would also testify to the bewilderment of the man trying to find his bearings with the fog starting to lift its veil and evaporate slowly. Where was he? And why was he there? These and such like questions teased his mind.

Abandoned at a deserted place, braving the buffets of chilly winds, flabbergasted, staggering, clutched by some hidden fear lurking in his heart, and not knowing where to go and from whom to seek succor, he intuitively took to a narrow track in the hope of reaching somewhere, village or town.

The old man, dazed and shocked, walked aimlessly, talking to himself. Tired and beaten by the biting cold, ambling forward with unstable steps, he sauntered on shakily. In the nerve-wracking wilderness, in a flashback, he remembered the nightmarish experience he had gone through and recalled his moorings.

He remembered that the kidnappers had admitted their guilt, and had promised that such a thing would not occur again. On the doctor's insistence, they took a solemn vow that they would do all the good they could, by all the means, in all the ways, at all the times, as long as ever they could. Before leaving him, the kidnappers put a 50-rupee note in his pocket to enable him to reach home. Two farmers, irrigating a field close by, heard him cry for help. They assisted him in stopping a bus and boarding it for Delhi. The money which the kidnappers had put into his pocket before releasing him, helped him return home, broken and exhausted, to narrate his story.

In a reversal of the situation, the captors emptied the purse and thus filled the heart of the doctor. The compassion and charity covered their sins. And the doctor forgave his captors for what they did, and for the promise they had made that they would not err again.

This reiterates our faith in the human heart which always remains human, full of innate goodness. One man is as true as another. One religion is as true as another. Those dehumanized quarrels for worldly riches, for pelf and power. They wrangle for religion. They write for it, speak for it, fight for it, die, kill and sin for it, anything but live for it. Evil communication corrupts good manners. But good company and good discourse not only arouse compassion, but warm cold hearts and bring about a change in the mindset. Therefore, we must trust that somehow good will be the final goal of ill, when man will be persuaded to say, "The world is my country, all mankind are my brethren, and to do good is my religion." Happy are men who believe that doing good and being good is the be-all and end-all of life.

CHAPTER XVII

Life Redeemed

The Railway Station was overcrowded with commuters, holiday picnickers, tourists and pilgrims, all waiting for the local shuttle. All of a sudden, there appeared on the scene, a young woman in her early thirties. She was quite good-looking, apparently affluent, neatly dressed in salwar- kameez, light-footed, copper-haired.

The crowd saw the damsel walking at ease in the middle of the rail track, oblivious of her surroundings like a philosopher, in a pensive mood, trampling the prickly stones underneath her feet. The setting seemed incongruous for one so fetching.

Suddenly, the clank of a train's wheels and the screech of its whistle were heard. Alarmed the crowd looked towards the fast-approaching train, then towards the lady walking with down-cast eyes towards her doom in the middle of the rails. People started shouting in unison: "Hey! Hey! Hey!"

The chorus of warning screams became more frenzied. But it failed to attract the attention of the woman who continued her walk lost in a world of her own.

Everybody stood petrified. Yes! Nobody from amongst the crowd including the railway cops at the station, dared risk his life for saving the woman's. The train rushed on, charging, nearer and nearer, whistling and whistling continuously. Passengers standing at the edge of the platform moved back a step or two.

There was jostling and pushing, empathetic hurrying hither and thither; everyone wishing the woman to be saved. But nobody knew what to do. Nobody, in fact, attempted to do anything, despite the gory death they were about to witness.

In this fear-charged pandemonium, from somewhere a middle-aged man in a black coat came charging and jumped onto the rails. Soon the train obscured him. His wife ran after him crying: "Vakil Sahib! Vakil Sahib! But Vakil Sahib had gone. Unable to bear the agony of her husband's act of courting death, she became delirious.

In a moment, the heart-stopping suspense was over. The gentleman in the black coat, an advocate, stood there holding the shaken woman as the train hurtled past.

Many from amongst the crowd patted, hugged and thanked the Good Samaritan, forgetting their own lack of courage a moment ago. I was also a witness to the whole scene. Ashamed of myself, I decided to dedicate this piece to him as a token of my personal thanksgiving.

The woman so rescued was deaf and dumb. She was crossing the rails as a shortcut to her house. What she did not know was that there was no shortcut to life, though there were many to death. When told with gestures that she was snatched away from the jaws of death, she looked blankly with her wild eyes at the crowd, then gave a grateful smile to the gentleman-saviour, babbled something, and walked off.

Whether the advocate could celebrate the day with a personal satisfaction, is not known. But the fact that he did give to a handicapped woman, a new lease of life as a gift, of course, made my day.

The incident reminded me of a couplet of Kabir, the famous saint-poet: *"Kabir woh nar pir hai, jo jane per pir / Jo per pir na janhiye, so kafir bepir"* (only he is a seer Kabir who knows others pain / Otherwise life is an existence, sinful, sorry and vain). Verily, the man who melts with social sympathy, though not allied, is of more worth than a thousand kinsmen, for we are all born for human love; it is the principle of existence and its only end.

CHAPTER XVIII

Who Learns from Innocence!

They were two youngsters, a brother and a sister. The boy aged 12 and the girl aged 15, were dressed spick and span in the school uniform. They were carrying satchels loaded with books at their backs and were waiting at the Bus Stop in Old Faridabad to catch an early morning bus for their school in Delhi. Their cherubic visages were eloquent of their respectable parents.

The youngsters were engrossed in mutual conversation oblivious to the crowd of commuters. Nevertheless, they registered their innocence and striking presence in the motley crowd. The crowd intermittently stole a look at the attractive children. They were stretching their necks and directing their searching gazes towards the farthest end of the road to see whether the bus was coming or not.

A Roadways Bus, bound for Chandigarh, arrived in time. The bus ploughed through the crowd, scattered the passengers helter-skelter, and came to a screeching halt. The commuters charged at the bus and scampered into it. In the flurry and scurry, the two children patiently waited for their turn. They were the last to board.

The youngsters occupied the seat in front of me. The girl handed over a 50-rupee note to me to pass it on to the conductor via other passengers for two tickets for Ashram, New Delhi. The note was handed over by commuters to the conductor, who in the same way dispatched the tickets and the balance amount back to the children.

The girl counted the balance returned by the conductor, looked at the value of the ticket, and counted the balance amount again. Discovering that the conductor had returned Rs 1.50 in excess, she directed the younger brother to return the excess amount to the conductor. The boy got up from his seat, slowly waded through the crowd of passengers, reached the conductor, and returned Rs 1.50. The conductor nodded his head in appreciation. All this while I watched the two urchins in admiration. And so did the crowd.

However, after some time the girl again started counting the money. On recalculation, she found that the conductor had in fact returned Rs 2.50 and not Rs 1.50 in excess. She once again asked her brother to go and return Re 1 more to the conductor. The boy as before obeyed his sister and returned another rupee to the conductor. The conductor reciprocated the honest children's comportment with a grateful smile.

The exemplary conduct of the children caused a susurration of approbation among the commuters who marvelled at the conscientious youngsters.

Spontaneously inspired by what impulse, I know not, I unpremeditatedly blessed the children and affectionately caressed their heads. The kids responded with "Thank you, uncle." Then they got down at Ashram, leaving us philosophizing about the moral 'sanskars' the children might have imbibed from their parents. Verily, wise and honest children make a glad father.

However, something antithetical happened at Gandhi-Samadhi on the Ring Road. When the Bus stopped at the red light, some passengers got down there. As soon as they alighted, the conductor demanded tickets, which they handed over to him, thinking that he wanted to check them, and in a huff crossed the road.

The conductor deposited the tickets in his pocket with the obvious intention of using them again on the onward journey to swindle the extra buck. And this happened in the full view of the passengers who raised many an eyebrow at the dramatic reversal of the situation. Soon the passengers disembarked at the ISBT, and went their way, passive, acquiescent, forgetful as always sans any remorse and blush of contempt.

Truly, morality is a private concern. And experience seldom learns from innocence.

CHAPTER XIX

Radha Needs Ghee More than Krishna

Des Raj has been washing and ironing our clothes. He had come to our town from his native village in Eastern UP years ago. I had helped him set up his 'jhuggy' in the vacant plot adjoining my house. Back home, he owned two acres of land. However owing to a lack of irrigation facilities, the land did not produce much to sustain his family. So, he had left his village, with his wife and two sons, in search of greener pastures. He and his wife washed clothes in the nearby 'Kothies,' and his sons ironed them. And they also washed cars in the morning. As their vocation prospered, he brought his two young daughters too. They worked as maidservants in the houses in the vicinity. Eventually, the family together could earn enough to spare.

Meanwhile, we were blessed with a grand-daughter. Since my wife and my daughter-in-law were working women, we were in search of a babysitter. My wife broached the topic with Des Raj. On his next visit to his village, he brought his youngest daughter, named Radha.

Radha was a little girl, just 9 in age. She was oval-faced, black in colour, small in stature, eyes wild, hair dishevelled, dressed in an over-sized frock, not washed for many days. Since the force of necessity was irresistible, my wife immediately employed her as a baby-sitter.

Soon Radha endeared herself to the whole family. My wife, a Headmistress of a school, was so pleased with her that she started teaching her. In three years, she had learnt the three R's and even could read the Hindi newspaper. Reciprocating the motherly gesture of my wife, Radha started doing additional work on her own. She dusted the house, regularly changed the bed sheets and the pillow covers, and helped my wife in the kitchen. She had almost become a member of our household. She took care of everything. We became entirely dependent upon her. Thus, we had a soothing present, bothering little for the morrow.

However, there is time for all things. The fleeting time touched her gently. She grew into an attractive young woman. Her father married her off to a boy from his native village. With Radha gone, our life became a jigsaw puzzle with most of the pieces missing. We had become so used to her that in her absence our routine of life was virtually paralyzed. But we were animated and elated when Radha returned after a few months.

As time passed, Radha gave birth to a baby-boy. In her absence, she asked her aunt to do our domestic work, till she was in fine fettle to return to her work. My wife visited her almost regularly to enquire about her health and the well-being of the baby. And amply provided her with milk-powder, 'desi ghee' etc., for her and her baby's nourishment.

As usual, after taking my bath, I readied myself for the daily pooja. I searched for desi ghee for the pooja lamp. But I could not find it. I asked my wife about it. She said that she had given the whole packet of desi ghee to Radha. I stared at her to understand what she meant. Sensing my discomfiture, she said: "Radha needed desi ghee more than your Lord Krishna." Then commented, "The love we bestow on our fellow-beings, is our own forever, which God returns to us in measures multiplied."

This little incident took me down the memory lane and reminded me of a story narrated by Leigh Hunt, a nineteenth-century British poet, in his poem "Abou Ben Adhem."

Once an angel appeared in Abou Ben Adhem's dream. He was writing something. Abou asked him as to what he was writing. The angel replied that he was preparing the list of those whom God loved. Abou enquired if his name was there. The angel replied in the negative. Abou then requested: "Write me as one who loves his fellow-beings."

The angel appeared again the next day. Abou again asked the same question. And the angel gave the same answer that he was short-listing the names of those God loved. Abou asked if his name was there. The angel said that Abou's name was there on top of the list, and conveyed the message that God loved those who loved their fellow-men.

Lord Krishna preached '*lokasamgraha*' (universal brotherhood and the interconnectedness of society), in the Gita (3.25). He advocated "*sarva bhuta hite ratah*," indulge yourself in the welfare of all creatures. And Lord Christ said, "Love thy neighbour as thyself." The gospels say that we should count no human foreign to us. When Socrates was, of what country he called himself, he said. "Of the world." Going by the dictum of Socrates, let us reiterate: "The world is my country, all mankind are my brethren, and to do good is my religion." When we see a man in woe, we should walk right up to him and say "hello", and be of help to him.

CHAPTER XX

Yudhishtra in the Election Fray: From Mahabharata to Bharata

The philosophy of life after death draws its sustenance from the *Gita* and the *Upanishads.* For example, Lord Krishna in the *Gita* propounds: "You and I, Arjuna, have lived many lives. I remember them all. You do not remember." (*Gita*: 4-5). And "just as a person casts off worn-out garments and puts on others that are new, even so does the embodied soul cast off worn-out bodies and take on others that are new." (*Gita*: 2.22).

The *Rig Veda* also abounds in such references: "When after death all the five elements dissolve among themselves, the *jivatma* (individual soul) remains, and this *Jivatma* takes to itself a new body." (5.6). Even the Bible raises the same question: "If a man dies, will he live again?" (*Book of Job, Old Testament*: 2).

Going by the aforementioned dictum of the holy scriptures, let us imagine that the Pandavas brothers have re-emerged from the eons of the hoary past at Indraprastha. And that they are advised by Lord Krishna, and persuaded by Balrama, to contest the elections to put the democracy of their Bharat back on the rails. Lord Krishna suggests that let Yudhishtra try his luck at the hustings, for he has the experience of being an administrator, a king as he has been in the past. Let us imagine that Yudhishtra is reborn. And he decides to contest elections in the present-day Indraprastha (that is Bharat). Duryodhana too is imagined to have been born in the present age, and he too tries to test his luck in the elections.

However, Yudhishtra is ignorant of the consequences he would be confronted with. There is no gainsaying the fact that the Pandavas would find the present-day socio-cultural and political scenario far different from that of the Mahabharata era. They would be appalled and dismayed to know that the politicians in the present-day Bharata have become specialists in the art of veiling, deceiving, and cheating. Even if they dissemble to speak the truth, the common populace does not believe them. Because the politicians now-a-days say the nastiest things in the nicest way.

There is a tall mansion-like building, all white and majestic. Outside this august and impressive edifice, have gathered a large number of people, all accoutred in white khadi, donning jackets of motley colours, white, blue, brown, pink, and yellow. Inside a room, are seated in the chairs around a big table, some senior leaders of a political party comprising the Election Panel. Their faces are recognizable.

On the walls of the spacious room are hung life-size portraits of Mahatma Gandhi and Jawahar Lal Nehru. They manifest a smile of hope. In the right-hand corner, silhouetted in the background, there is a bronze statue with three monkeys, one refusing to see, the other adamant not to hear, and the third determined not to speak. But the leaders have turned their backs towards them. They are obviously oblivious of them. They are sifting a pile of papers, which look like applications and bio-data of the prospective candidates aspiring to contest elections.

In the porch outside the room are sitting the ticket-seekers. Among them, sitting on a bench, is Yudhishtra. He is empty-handed, with just a paper, perhaps his bio-data, protruding out of his pocket. On the other side of the row of benches, is seated Duryodhana. He has a briefcase resting upon his lap. His face reflects a gleam of confidence and a glimmer of a politician well-versed in the art of hypocrisy and dissembling. After a prolonged discussion and mutual susurrus, the Election Panel decides in unison to interview the prospective candidates. Yudhishtra is the first to be called. Then ensues an interesting question-answer session.

(Yudhishtra enters the committee room. With folded hands, he respectfully bows his head and greets the members. As we know him from the Mahabharata era, this gesture, a part of his characteristic attributes, was obviously expected of him. Pointing towards the chair,

the President signals Yudhishtra to sit).

President: What is your name? Yes! It is there in the application. Yudhishtra ! Well, Mr Yudhishtra! Please tell us what is your popular base? We have gone through your bio-data, and this vital fact is nowhere mentioned.

Yudhishtra: Sir! I am a follower of righteousness. I am known by the nickname *'Dharamraja,* not only in Indraprastha but also in the whole of the Aryavrata.

President: (*Smiling at the quaint reply, the president of the Election Panel further asks*). Not Dharam. I want to know your popular base vis-à-vis your caste and clan. How many of them are the voters in Indraprastha?

Yudhishtra: Honourable Sir! We are five brothers; each a paragon of virtue and valour.

President: Only five! That is your muscle power!

Yudhishtra: Sir! you don't know their prowess. Arjun is the best archer in the whole of Aryavrat. Bhim personifies great power and strength, unparalleled in the whole world. This is my muscle power unmatched even in the best of warriors.

President: Are you referring to that Arjuna who disguised himself as Brihanla, and clapped like a eunuch to save his life? Many Brihanlas have already become members of our party, and even won elections. That is no merit to garner votes. And about Bhima, the less said the better. He disguised himself as a cook and maintained a façade of dissembling to hoodwink.

However, tell us. In order to protect Arjuna, will your mother succeed in procuring *kawach* (protecting gear) and *kundal* (ear-rings) of Karna, even in the coming electoral battle? Further, do you have any glamorous woman to attract electorates in the election campaign? Do you have some such tale that may fetch sympathy votes?

Yudhishtra: Sir! We have Draupaddi, the wife of five brothers. Her *cheer-haran* (disrobing) by Duryodhana and Dushasan would be made an issue to secure sympathy votes. (*However, Yudhishtra turned a deaf ear to the Karna's Kawach and Kundal question).*

President: Draupadi! One wife of five brothers. What kind of *dharam* is this, Dharamraj? We want a *kulvadhu* (virtuous woman of a noble family) and not a *nagarvadhu* (a sort of courtesan). And at the time of *cheer-haran*, all the five brothers, warriors great by whom you so often swear, they sat quietly with their heads down, and did not protest: they did not even engender confidence by way of making a statement of condemnation. You could not make an issue then. How would you make an issue now after so many centuries!

Even otherwise clothes are no longer an issue these days. Many scantily clad women are already members of our party, and even have been elected as legislators. Therefore, for our party *cheer-haran* could not be an election issue. Tell us some other vote-garnering issue!

Yudhishtra: The great Bhisham Pitamah, Kakashri Vidur, Kulguru Kripacharya, and Guru Dronacharya, have all extended their moral support to us. They are certainly big names to impress and influence the electorates.

President: This is electoral Mahabharata, and not a platform for discourse on *nitishastra* (ethics). We want the active participation of the popular leaders in the election campaign. All these big names are of no use to us in the elections. Those who gave you only moral support in the battle with the Kauravas, will not serve any electoral purpose now. Our party in the elections does not need any moral support, but actual and active support.

Yudhishtra: *Disheartened Yudhishtra played the last 'chal' (move) on the 'chauser (dice-board):* "Sir! we have the blessings of Lord Krishna."

President: *Bursting into a horse laugh, the President, in the tone of an opinionated person, said:* "Son! you are ignorant about the present-day political situation and social reality. Today, the political issue is not Krishna. It is Rama. When you get the blessings of Rama, then come to us for the ticket. In that eventually, we may consider your application favourably. We are sorry! You don't fit in the electoral strategy of our party."

The Secretary of the Screening Committee then rang the bell and asked the peon to call in Duryodhana. Prince Duryodhana walks into the Committee Room with his usual mannerisms: vanity, boast and pretension personified. Before the President of the Election Panel asks Duryodhana to sit down in the chair, Duryodhana, literally throws his briefcase -- which he was carrying -- on the table with a bang.

President: *(Surprised, the President asks)*: "What is this?"

Duryodhana: (*He straightens himself, displays a winning smile on his face, and erupts into a peal of laughter; clearing his throat, he replies in his heavy voice*): "Sire! here are 500 gold coins for the party. Accept my contribution."

(*The members of the Election Committee, looked at each other with gleeful smile. They rolled their eyes here and there, nodded their heads in appreciation, beckoned the peon, and with a wave of hand indicated to him to take the briefcase inside*). Then thus they proceeded with the interview.

President: Duryodhana! History has it that Indraprastha was ruled by the Pandavas, and not by the Kauravas. We don't think, you, as the Kaurava chieftain, made any mark, politically, socially, and culturally, and created any popular base.

Duryodhana: (*Duryodhana raises his eyebrows, and asks in his usual garrulous voice*):

"Base! What is that thing?" And himself answers the point: "Elections are not won on the basis of any base, but with money and muscle power. And I have both of them. In the Indraprastha constituency, there are not as many polling booths as the number of my brothers. I have one hundred brothers. If one brother 'manages,' yes 'manages', one polling booth, yet several of my brothers will still remain surplus.

President: Duryodhana! How many musclemen do you have?

Duryodhana: Do you think one hundred are less? Each of my brothers is a wrestler. Then I have many other princes, progenies of those kings and potentates who had helped us in the Mahabharata War. Besides, Karna, the great archer, is my all-weather friend.

President: But Sir, Karna is famous for his charity! That is why he is called "Danveer Karan." If Mata Kunti once again seeks his *kawach* (protecting gear) and*kundal* (ear-rings), then you are sure to lose the whole battle, the way you lost in the Mahabharata War.

Duryodhana: (*Waving his heavy mace in the air*) Gone are those days. Times are different now. The idiosyncrasies of the people have undergone a complete metamorphosis, as also the priorities. Karan has become wiser, and more sagacious. Karan will not commit the mistake he committed during the Great War. He has learnt a lot from his past experience. Yet, in the eventuality Mata Kunti insists on *kawach* and *kundal*, then we have the Gafar Market. Karan can buy a duplicate *kawach* and *Kundal* and give it to his unwary and credulous mother.

(*The members of the Committee were taken aback at the audacity and ready-wit of Duryodhana, and the confidence his face manifested. The Secretary looked towards the President, and spoke in a hush-hush voice in his ears*).

Secretary: "Sir, he is a useful man!"

President: (*The President shook his head in approval*): Yes! this is true that you have a lot of muscle power with which you will succeed in bogus voting, as also in booth capturing. But to succeed as a politician, one needs to have strategy, political philosophy and a bit of diplomacy. Do you have any person, who, like a statesman, has these qualities, essential for winning an election?

Duryodhana: (*Duryodhan heaved a long sigh. With a mischievous glint in his eyes and a Machiavellian smile on his face, he pitied the lack of common sense of the Committee members. He blurts out*): Sire! don't you know that Shakuni is not only my maternal uncle but also my mentor, philosopher and guide! And in the entire Aryavrat, there is no bigger strategist and intriguer than Shakuni. (*Caressing his long whiskers with his fingers, he further adds*): You must know that "Uncle Shakuni, when he rubs *pasas* (pawns) of the *chausar* (dice board) in his hands, then many stalwarts remain awe-struck at the excellent throw on the dice. He is such a person who can manipulate defeat into victory, *alpmat* (minority) into *bahumat*, i.e. majority. History has it that he has won many an electoral battle through his machinations. Uncle Shakuni will be my Election Manager."

President: But Duryodhan, you disrobed Draupaddi. If the opposition makes it an electoral issue, then not only your election but the election of the entire Aryavrat, will be jeopardized.

Duryodhan: *Raising his eyebrows like a big bully, he shamelessly points out:* "Sire! who cares for the incident of disrobing now-a-days? It could not become an issue then, when the incident happened in the distant past; how will it become an issue now? The common populace has a very short memory. Moreover, incidents of disrobing of women happen day in and day out these days, and no longer become any news. Nor do such incidents remain in the news for long in the print and electronic media. Therefore, the disrobing of Draupadi will neither be an issue, nor any news, in the coming elections.

President: But you are notorious as a criminal, as a goon, as a terrorizing bully. And as such owing to your criminal background, your nomination is likely to be challenged by your rivals, and in that eventuality, it is likely to be cancelled by the Election Commission.

Duryodhana: What nonsense! Who dares give evidence against me? And when there is no evidence, there is no case, and as such there is no crime. (*Before the President could ask the next question*), Duryodhana asserted, "Listen to me, Mr President! Tatshri Bhishm Pitamah will campaign for me. And when he campaigns and supports me, the entire Aryavrat will fall in line."

Secretary: (*At this point of the interview, the Secretary of the Election Panel, intervenes*). "But the moral support of Bhisham Pitamah is with the Pandavas. Besides, he is lying on the bed of arrows, how would he campaign for you?"

Duryodhana: (*Duryodhana, dissembling seriousness like a seasoned and well-groomed politician, points out*). Bhisham Pitamah had taken a vow, and given a word to his father that he would be loyal to the Hastinapur throne. And since I am a prince of Hastinapur, therefore, he is bound by his vow to support me.

Further, we will politically exploit Pitamah's lying on the bed of arrows, waiting for death. Since Pitamah was made to lie supine on the bed of arrows by Arjuna, we would make that an issue, propagate it and garner sympathy votes. And we have another plus point. The great Sanjay, bestowed with the divine eyes by Rishi Ved Vyas, who narrated the *Mahabharata* story live to my father, King Dhritrashtra, will do the necessary election propaganda in my favour.

President: But Sanjay was an official communicator, a King's broadcaster. How can he be a campaigner for an individual?

Duryodhana: What is official about it! I will manipulate everything. I will find a way and hoodwink the Election Commission.

(The members of the Election Committee, then, go into a huddle, and discuss the electoral prospects of Duryodhana among themselves. After that the President announces the result).

President: Duryodhana. We are not only fully satisfied with your interview but also pleased with you. You have all the virtues of a leader and the qualities of a successful politician. Therefore, we have decided to recommend your name to the High Command to give you the party ticket to contest the election from the Indraparstha Constituency. May God bless you!

From what is aforementioned, it stands substantiated that Yudhishtra of the Mahabharata was quite different from Yudhishtra of Bharata. It is a difference between then and now, of incompatibility of the socio-political ambience of the hoary past with that of today. According to the mythical history, the Mahabharata Yudhishtra personifies righteousness; he epitomizes truth, virtue and ethical qualities. As such, he continues to follow his characteristic qualities even in the modern Bharata. He has not changed. He remains immutable. Consequently, Yudhishtra of the historical past finds himself a misfit, a failure, in the present-day socio-political and cultural ambience. On the other hand, Duryoddhana who represents unrighteousness, remains as unscrupulous and unprincipled even in the present times as he was during the Mahabharata era. Therefore, he finds himself acceptable in the present-day socio-political atmosphere.

Interestingly, Yudhishtra who had answered all the questions of the Yaksha in the *Mahabharata*, and had ultimately succeeded in bringing his dead brothers back to life, failed to give satisfactory answers to the questions of the lesser mortals, and thus appeared to be insufficient in getting the ticket for contesting the election. Not only that, he even gets a severe drubbing at the hands of the members of the Election Panel. He is unable to convince them about his uprightness and virtues. The Election Panel cannot see the difference between dharma and adharma. The story of the riddle-contest between Yudhishtra and the Yaksha appears in the *Vana Parva* of the *Mahabharata*.

Furthermore, in the book, in the *Vana Parva*, Yudhishtra has an encounter with a huge python. The python is, in fact, king Nahusha, one of the ancestors of the Pandavas. Here too Yuddhishtraa successfully answers all the questions of Nahusha, and gets his brother Bhima released from the stranglehold of the Python.

There is no gainsaying the fact that Yudhishtra of the *Mahabharata*, manifests his dexterity to satisfy both the Yaksha and Nahusha with his equitable and righteous answers. But the same Yudhishtra fails to answer the questions in the manner and to the extent expected of him by the members of the Election Committee. The reasons are not far to seek.

Webster's Dictionary defines two types of politicians. One -who is experienced in the art and science of government, and the other -who is primarily interested in political gains and narrow selfish interests. We have lost down the decades the politician of the first type. It is the second type of politician who rules the roost, who has downgraded democracy as the government 'off' the people, 'far' the people and 'buy' or 'bye' (goodbye) the people. Yudhishtra belongs to the political class of the first type, and Duryodhana to the politics of the second kind which connotes that politics these days has become symptomatic of the game of scheming, cunning, hiding, veiling, hypocrisy, crime, lies, manipulation and self-aggrandizement. Shakespeare nicknames such politicians as "scurvy politicians," obviously a speaking sobriquet. The new political class is different from their predecessors, qua the politicians of the past era. That is why Yudhishtra is a misfit in the given socio-political ambience, for he remains steadfast in his characteristic idiosyncrasies, and has not changed with the passage of time. Hence the journey of Yudhishtra from Mahabharata to Bharata, from success to failure.

CHAPTER XXI

God's Grace

Last Sunday I went to a grocery store to buy some provisions. As I was climbing the stairs, I heard a big bang of a loud crash. As soon as I entered the store, I sauntered towards the sound. There was a group of people huddled together, whispering and looking at each other in awe. When I walked up to the scene of occurrence, I saw a middle-aged lady lying on the ground. Soon I came to know that the lady who had come to the grocery store to buy some provisions, per chance slipped and bumped into a glass showcase with her cart. The glass showcase filled with dishes and glass-ware, fell on her. It was broken into smithereens. The glass pieces were scattered all around. The woman was also hurt by the glass shards and was bleeding from her forehead.

Somehow, she managed to extricate herself from underneath the fallen showcase and stood up on her tottering legs. Feeling embarrassed by the mishap, she kneeled on the floor in order to pick up the shattered pieces. Her husband, in the meantime, picked up the broken dishes and other glass wares. He was frantically peeling off the bar- code from each broken dish and glass ware. He loudly told his wife: "Darling, I think you are not seriously hurt. Don't worry. We will pay for the loss the owner of the grocery shop has suffered."

I, too, was standing there with the crowd of people, and silently watching the disconcerting incident. I felt so bad for the lady, especially when I saw a large number of people gathered there, and staring at the lady and glass shards scattered all over. But none of them came to her help. They were just onlookers. However, the human in me could not resist and restrain me from coming to her aid. I walked up to the lady, knelt beside her, and began to pick up the broken pieces. Suddenly the awoken conscience in me manifested itself in the human compassion and sympathy. I caressed her head and said: "Respected mother! Please don't feel uneasy and upset. What has happened has happened." And I started helping her pick up the scattered pieces.

Just then came running the Manager of the Store. He knelt beside us and joined us in picking up the broken pieces. He said: "Please leave it. We will clean this up." With a humane touch, he made the woman stand up, and with commiseration and tender-heartedness, writ large on his brow, he called his minions. "Take this graceful lady to the hospital, and have that cut on her forehead looked at." Nevertheless, the woman was totally confused and flustered by this kind of loving and caressing treatment. She said: "Before going to the hospital, I must pay for all this first." However, the Manager smiled a gracious smile and helped the woman to her feet. "No ma'am! We have insurance for this. You do not have to pay anything for this loss."

Verily, we all have the same insurance, which is called "GRACE." And when we accept God as our Lord and Saviour, and ask for forgiveness from the Manager of the universe, the Master of the World will say: "Everything has already been paid for. Go on your way. You are free; you are forgiven." Let us imagine God meting out the same treatment to us. Let us collect the broken pieces of heart from all the disappointments, the buffets, and the blows, that the life has thrown at us. God will heal all the wounds, who will, willy-nilly, forgive our sins and mistakes.

CHAPTER XXII

Tale Told by the Buddha

One day, Gautam Buddha was meditating under a tree. Just then he was approached by a young girl, named Sujata. She presented a bowl full of milk-rice. The Buddha ate the milk-rice, and then tossed the empty bowl into the river flowing nearby. The bowl floated. This was the signal that the moment of triumph was at hand.

The Buddha left that spot and placed himself under the Bo tree, where he attained enlightenment, and redeemed the whole world. There he was approached by Kama-Mara, the god of love and death. At his sight the protecting deities of the universe took flight. Kama-Mara tried hard to disturb the concentration of the Buddha. But the Buddha remained unmoved. Mara then deployed his daughters, Desire, Pining and Lust, but the Buddha's mind could not be distracted. The Buddha had overcome the Kama (love and lust), and Mara (death).

The word Kama, standing for *Kamdeva*, that is, the god of love, has its origin in the word "*kam*" which, literally means "desire." In fact, *kam* or desire is the root of all evils, that is *kam, krodh, lobh, moh, ahankara,* which Lord Krishna in the Gita wanted Arjuna to discard. The desire for sex, or lust, is "kam." Nonfulfillment of desire and when things do not happen as planned, thought, or desired leads to "krodh," that is anger. Desire for money becomes "lobh" (greed); desire for love for parents, children, and other kith and kin, is "moh," and desire to rule and suppress the world, valuing oneself more than others on grounds of qualities, rank and possession, results in "ahankara" (self-sense, or phenomenal ego). Thus, we see that "kam" is the symbol, or attribute of love, lust and desire. Desire leads to degradation and suffering. Successful overcoming of lust or desire clears the way to self-realization, or "nirvana." The root meaning of "nirvana" is blowing out--that is extinguishing-- the fire of desire.

Arjuna asks Lord Krishna

"By what is man impelled to commit sin, as if by force, even against his will?"

The Gita: 3:36

Krishna replies: "This is craving (desire), this is wrath, born of the mode of passion, all-devouring and the most sinful. Know this to be the enemy here.

The Gita 3:37

Dr S. Radhakrishnan's Translation

Desire is never satisfied by the enjoyment of the objects of desire; it grows more and more as does the fire to which fuel is added. Therefore, man has to destroy this fire of "desire" by wisdom (*vivek*), discrimination, and righteous (good) karmas (actions).

Now the question arises: "What is karma?" The answer to this question was given by Gautam Buddha. One day the Buddha was sitting with his disciples. One of the disciples asked him: "What is Karma?" The Buddha answered this question by narrating a story.

In the hoary past, there was a king. Once he was touring his kingdom on his elephant. Suddenly, he stopped in front of a shop in the market, and said to his Minister, accompanying him: "I don't like the face of this shopkeeper. I want to hang him. I don't know, why such a feeling, such an idea, has come to my mind?" The Minister was shocked to hear these words. But before he could ask the king "why did he utter such words," the king had moved on.

The next day, the Minister decided to visit the shop incognito to know the reason behind the king's rant. He disguised himself in the garb of a local denizen so that he could not be recognized. He asked the shopkeeper in an intimate tone: "Brother, how is your business faring?" The shopkeeper was a sandalwood merchant. He lamented his dwindling business. He said in a depressed tone; "There is hardly any customer these days. People do come to my shop, smell the fragrance of the sandalwood, ask for the price, and then go away. They would even praise the quality of the sandalwood, but would not buy even a piece or two. My only wish is that the king should die soon. Then there would be a huge demand for the sandalwood for his last rites." As he is the only sandalwood merchant, the king's death would mean a windfall.

The Minister, a wise and experienced administrator, understood as to why the king had stopped in front of his shop, and expressed a desire to hang the shopkeeper. Perhaps the vibration emanating out of the negative thoughts of the sandalwood merchant had subtly affected the king's psyche, qua subconscious, who had in turn nurtured the same kind of negative thought arising within.

The Minister, without revealing his identity as to who he was and what happened a day before, expressed his desire to buy some pieces of sandalwood. The shopkeeper was mighty pleased as he had got a customer after many days. He wrapped the sandalwood neatly and handed over the bundle to the Minister. With the pieces of the sandalwood in hand, the Minister straight away came to the court. The king was sitting on his throne. The Minister offered him the Sandalwood, saying that this rare sandalwood had been sent to him by the shopkeeper as a gift. The king was, literally amazed. When he opened the bundle, he was pleasantly surprised by the fine golden colour of the sandalwood, and the agreeable fragrance coming out of it. The king felt sorry in his heart that he had harboured ill thought to hang him. Such thoughts were unbecoming of a king. In order to expiate for his malignant desire, he sent some gold coins to the merchant.

When the shopkeeper received the bounty of gold coins from the king, he too was astounded and felt sorry for desiring the death of his monarch. He then vociferously proclaimed the virtues of the king who was munificent and bountiful. He pronounced that as he was on the brink of penury, the king sent the gold coins, and thus saved him. He soon became oblivious of the morbid thoughts he had felt towards the king, and even repented for having entertained such negative feelings, and ill-intention, just for personal benefits, for selfish motives. When one has a good and kind thought for another person, that positive thought would come back in a constructive, optimistic and favourable manner. But, if one entertains evil thoughts, those thoughts will bounce back as retribution, as revenge and requital.

Then the Buddha asked his disciples: "What is Karma?" Many disciples replied: "Our words, our deeds, our feelings, are symptomatic of our karma, our actions." Gautama Buddha shook his head, and explicated: "Your thoughts are your Karma."

CHAPTER XXIII

God Responds to Prayers

Hari Krishan, a renowned doctor, was scheduled to participate in an important conference of eminent medicos in Lucknow. He was to catch the afternoon flight from New Delhi. Despite the best efforts to reach the airport in time, he got late. The reason for the delay was a large number of patients that he attended to in the OPD in the Hospital where he was working. However, when he reached the airport, he hurriedly got down from his chauffeur-driven car and rushed to catch the flight which was ready to leave. He boarded the flight, sat down in his seat, and the flight took off. The aircraft was in the air for about an hour, when it started raining heavily. The wind too blew at the turbulent speed. Suddenly, the radio system in the plane went out of order. The captain of the plane announced that since the radio system in the plane was not working, he was perforce compelled to land at the nearby airport. As soon as the plane landed, Doctor Hari Krishan came out of the plane. He vociferously complained to the captain that he was to attend an important conference, and as such every minute of his time was precious. It was essential for him to attend the conference of prominent Surgeons who would be arriving there to attend the conference from all over the globe.

There was a passenger who was standing nearby. He recognized Doctor Hari Krishan. He said: "Doctor! I know you, your reputation and your expertise, as I have been your patient. Lucknow is only a two-hour journey from here by road. You can hire a Taxi and reach your destination in time. The conference, as you say, would take place in the evening. By that time, you would reach the venue of the conference by road. Dr Hari Krishna thanked the co-passenger for the suggestion. He immediately hired a Taxi and decided to make the journey by road speedily. But unfortunately, it rained cats and dogs; in fact, it was a fierce storm. It became well-nigh impossible for the Taxi driver to ply the vehicle in such an inclement weather. Notwithstanding the bad weather, the driver, goaded by the doctor, continued to ply the vehicle. Soon the driver lost the way. In order to find the way, he stopped the car in front of a house, situated in a sparsely inhabited hamlet in an isolated place. He knocked at the door.

From inside the room came a feeble voice: "Please come in. The weather is rough and squally. Please take shelter inside the room." The doctor opened the door and entered into the room. Inside was sitting an aged woman reciting some verses from the Gita. The doctor said: "Mata Ji! If you don't mind, may I use your phone?" The elderly lady smiled. She pointed out: "Son, what phone! Here there is neither electricity nor any phone." Nevertheless, she advised Doctor Hari Krishan: "There is *charnamrit* in that copper cup. Please sip it. You will feel better. It will relieve you of your fatigue, and exhaustion. There are some fruits in that basket. You can eat them and allay your hunger. It will help you cover the rest of your journey with ease."

The doctor, the worldly-wise person as he was, did not know much about the *charnamrit*. He asked the woman about it. The old lady informed me that the "*charnamrit* was a kind of sacred nectar coming from God's feet. It simply means that the sacred elixir of Lord Krishna's feet is the demolisher of all sins. Moreover, it is a sort of medicine, and if you consume *charnamrit*, you would feel better spiritually and morally. Furthermore, in *charnamrit* are mixed the basil (*tulsi*) leaves, and it is kept in a copper vessel, which proliferates its medicinal properties."

The doctor thanked the benign lady. When he was about to drink *charnamrit*, he perchance espied a small child, wrapped in a blanket, and sleeping close to the lady. The aged woman caressed the child at short intervals. In the meanwhile, the old lady had finished the reading of holy verses from the Gita. Then the doctor asked: "Mother, your humane behaviour has impressed me a lot. Your characteristic idiosyncrasies have virtually bewitched me. Please pray for me that the rain stops, and I am enabled to resume the journey to reach the conference venue in time. I am sure your prayer would certainly be accepted by Lord Krishna." The lady said: "Son, there is nothing like this. You are my guest. And to serve an Atithi (guest) is God's commandment. Since I am a staunch devotee of Krishna, to serve an Atithi, as also human beings in distress, is my Lord's diktat. I have prayed for you too. Lord Krishna has always responded to my prayers, so benign and kind, He has been. There is yet another prayer which Krishana might hear and respond."

The doctor asked: "Mother, what is that prayer?" The old woman replied: "This four-year-old child who is lying half-dead in front of you, is my grandson. Both his mother and father have died. It is enjoined on me, in my old age, to look after him. The doctors say that he is suffering from some strange disease. They have shown their inability to treat this child, for they lack the expertise to treat this strange ailment. However, they have repeatedly suggested to me that there is a well-known doctor – what is his name, yes, I recall—he is Doctor Hari Krishan, who can operate upon this child and cure him of the disease. How can I locate Doctor Hari Krishna? And even if I am able to reach him, he may or may not treat my grandson. I pray to Krishna day in and day out to intervene and do something tangible for the treatment of the ailing child. As is implied in the name of the doctor Hari Krishan, he must be an emissary, the representative of the Lord. It is only Krishna who can ease my predicament."

Hearing the woeful tale of the aged woman, tears wallowed in the eyes of Hari Krishna. With a choked voice, he said: "Mother! I am Doctor Hari Krishna. Obviously, Krishna has responded to your prayer. Verily, it is Krishna who has compelled me to alight from the plane. It is Krishna who caused black clouds to pour down water on the earth, and impede my journey to Lucknow. It is again Krishna who has brought me to your hut, for it is He who comes to the aid of his devotees when man becomes helpless and hapless. Willy-nilly, I happen to be the herald, the errand-man, the harbinger of Lord Krishna. May God bless you, your grandson and every mortal! I need not go to Lucknow to participate in the conference. God has given me a great task, rather a yeoman mission, to operate upon this child and save his life." The old lady, with tears in her eyes, cried in gratitude. It was a cry of gratitude to Lord Krishna. She expressed her gratefulness both to Lord Krishna, and his benign emissary.

There is no gainsaying the fact that more things are wrought by prayer than the world dreams of. For prayers are God's blessings. Only God knows what is good for his devotees. Verily, honest prayers are always answered.

CHAPTER XXIV

Krishna and Christ: Where the East West Meet

Lord Krishna is the god of many splendours. And so is Lord Christ. Both descended to the earth with the same purpose to raise man to a higher grade of life and redeem mankind. The Supreme, though unborn and undying, reveals Himself in human embodiment to overthrow the forces of ignorance and selfishness, to replace hatred and cruelty with love and mercy, and to supplant unrighteousness with righteousness.

The scriptures of the East and the West, though remote in time, are not remote in thought. Since the human nature is immutable, therefore they are relevant to all times. They disclose the working of the primal impulses of the human soul, cutting across the differences of race and geographical boundaries.

The Sanskrit word "Upanishad" is a synthesis of *up-ni-shad:* 'up' means under, 'ni' means beneath, or nether, and 'shad' means to sit near. The whole word would then mean sitting at the feet of the maser. In the Vedic age, a group of pupils sat near the teacher to learn from him the secret doctrines.

When one reads in the Gospels that Jesus went "up into a mountain: and when he was set, his disciples came unto him," one can imagine them sitting at the feet of their Master. And the whole Sermon on the Mount might be considered as an Upanishad. Further, the root of the word 'gospel', in old or middle English, is 'godspel,' which means 'god' (good) plus 'spell' (tale). So, the gospel, in general, means the message or teachings of a religious teacher. Therefore, there are interesting similarities between the gospels and the Apostle-teachers of the East and the West.

For example, both the Upanishads and the Bible were written on the scrolls made of papyrus plant, that is *"bhoj Patra."* In fact, the Bible literally means "papyrus book." And Lord Krishna and Lord Christ, the Apostle-Teachers, though born in different times, in different climes, the twain have interesting similarities in their lives and precepts.

Kansa, the King of Mathura, and Herod, the King of Palestine, were forewarned that they would be killed by a child. So, they slaughtered children mercilessly. But as divinity ordained, Krishna and Christ had miraculous births. Krishna was born in captivity. And Christ was born in a manger. Immediately after birth, Christ was taken to Goshel in Egypt. Vasudeva used a basket, a prototype of the manger, to transport Krishna to Gokul. By implication, Goshel in Egypt is a reverberation of Gokul in India. The favourite bird of Christ is the dove, while that of Krishna is 'garuda', and of Vishnu is the eagle. "Yahudah" in Hebrew is the distortion of Yadu (Vansha) in Sanskrit. Similarly, Vasudev is equivalent to Yusef. The Christians and the Greeks spell 'Christ' as 'krist', or 'chris', and the Hindus write Krishna as 'chrisna.'

Christ means the Anointed One. Jesus signifies the Savior. Jesus Christ came into the world to save mankind. And so did Lord Krishna who preached *loksangraha* - universal brotherhood, (Gita 3.25), "*sarva bhuta hite ratah*", indulge yourself in the welfare of all creatures. Similarly. Lord Christ said, "Love thy neighbour as thyself."

Krishna is from the root "krish", which means to scrape, because he scrapes, or draws away all sins and other sources of evil from his devotees. He who attracts all, or arouses devotion in all is, Krishna: "*karshati sarvam karshnah*." Christ, the 'Anointed One' and the 'Savior" redeemed mankind and transformed the sinners. In fact, both were the moral teachers, who taught the world the dignity of human life.

Krishna and Christ were basically pacifists. But they also resorted to violence to destroy sin and evil. Thus, they were a synthesis of a lamb (as Christ is called), and a tiger. In the *Mahabharata,* Krishna makes all efforts to avoid war. He even asks for five villages for the Pandavas. But Duryodhana refuses. Krishna then advocates and also participates in the Great War. Lord Christ, in the "Sermon on the Mount" preaches humility, peace and non-violence. But the same Christ in the War in Heaven, pursues Satan down to the hell (called "Harrowing of the Hell") and destroys him.

The vision of the Cosmic Form that Krishna reveals in Chapter 11 of the Gita, has its echoes in the Bible too. "Behold, O Partha (Arjuna) my forms, a hundred-fold, a thousand-fold, various in kind, divine, of various colours and shapes" (11.5). "I behold Thee as one without beginning, middle or end, of infinite power... with the moon and the Sun as thine eyes, with Thy face as a flaming fire, whose radiance burns this universe" (11.9). Arjuna loses his bearings. The tremendous experience has in it the elements of surprise and rapture. This celestial vision, of all in one, is not a myth, or a legend, but a spiritual experience.

Reminiscent of Krishna's divine revelation, is the transfiguration of Jesus in the New Testament (Mark:2-8): "Six days later Jesus took with him Peter, James, and John, and led them up a high mountain, where they were alone. As they looked on, a change came over Jesus, and his clothes became shining white." Peter spoke up and said to Jesus: "Teacher, how good it is that we are here!" .... "He and others were so frightened that he did not know what to say."

Again, in Revelation (4), we have a glimpse of the cosmic vision: "There in heaven was a throne with someone sitting on it. His face gleamed like such precious stones as jasper and carnelian .... From the throne came the flashes of lightning, rumblings and peals of thunder ... Surrounding the throne on each of its sides, were four living creatures .... Day and night they never stopped singing .... Holy, holy, holy, is the Lord God Almighty, who was, who is, and who is to come."

There is no gainsaying the fact both Lord Krishna and Lord Christ were the manifestations of the same divinity, separated only by time and space. Their precepts and teachings were the same yesterday, are the same today, and will remain the same forever. Though our sages are receding from us, yet time has no power over the names, deeds and words of our Apostle-teachers.

CHAPTER XXV

Bhagwan Uvach

(*Bhagwan Spoke Thus*)

He is Bhagwan. Don't be surprised! He is not Bhagwan incarnate. His is a mere mortal, Bhagwan Dass, three-score-and-ten, a superannuated middle-rank bureaucrat, blear-eyed, slightly muddled. Wrinkles might be written on his face, but not on his heart. Notwithstanding his old age, he is as livelier and chirpy as a lark, cutting jokes with sexual overtones, and making fun of his aged friends. In fact, his jokes do not have any rancour. They are satires aimed at caricature and lampooning of his co-strollers who gather in the park for a walk. And I am no exception. He laughs with me, quite often laughs at me. So animated and spirited, vivacious and vibrant, is he.

My daily interaction with him makes me think that the aged people, by and large, bring with them the experience and wisdom that they have gathered over the years. Quite often I ask myself: "Does the old age bring metamorphosis, transmutation? Yes, it does. For, the age changes the idiosyncrasies of a man. His attitude to life undergoes transformation. His intercourse, his communion, with fellow human beings, becomes symptomatic of mutability."

Every day in the evening I go to a park, situated close to my house. There I meet a group of old people, superannuated antiques, though not outdated. Most of them are retired government officials, army officers and other professionals. Last evening, I asked my friend, Bhagwan Dass, as to what sort of changes he was feeling in him. "Has his comprehension, his insight vis-a-vis his life from then when he was young and now, changed for the better, or the worse?" He raised his eyebrows, ruminated for a while, and then revealed interesting aspects of life. What he divulged could be a salubrious lesson for all aged citizens, popularly called senior citizens.

Bhagwan Dass *uvach* (said): "Life is a long lesson in humility; it is an art of drawing sufficient conclusions from insufficient premises." He averred that when he was young, he had thought that life was beautiful. In the spring of life, a young man's fancy turns to love. Then he believed that "youth" knew everything, and as such was confident in his assertions. Then the blood was warmer. "But as the years passed, and I became old, and was given the epithet of "senior citizen," I became wiser, and could succinctly see the difference between the youth and age. The excesses of youth were supplanted by the enlightened and rational perception, which age brought into its vogue. The pranks and naughtiness of youthful days have been replaced by sobriety, pragmaticism, and restraint. I have now become more sagacious. A different perception of life has dawned on me. In the heyday of my life, I loved my parents, my spouse, and my progenies. I had the erroneous belief that I am all in all of my family and that the well-being of my family rests on me. Then my young friends arranged parties where each one of us resorted to jests appertaining our colleagues, more particularly to the female colleagues. But that is passe now. I now love myself. I have belatedly realised that I am not Atlas (a Titan who was forced by Zeus, the Chief of gods in the Greek mythology) to support the heaven on his shoulder. I am now convinced that the world does not rest on my shoulders. And that it is no longer my responsibility to care for the welfare, safety and security of my kith and kin."

Bhagwan disclosed that in his old age, "I have become more practical, more judicious, more discerning, more humane and prudent. I no longer bargain, nay haggle, with vegetable and fruit vendors. I now think that to pay a little more to the street vendors, would not make any big dent into my pocket. Paying a little more to a poor person might help the impoverished vendor save some money for the fee of his school-going daughter."

He further stated that invariably "he paid to the Taxi driver, and walked off. He did not wait for the return of the change (balance). The extra money might bring a smile on his face. This might help him live with ease, and assuage his hard toil a little. After all, he toiled much harder for a living than a me-like person." He further added that he had stopped telling his friends that he had already heard the story narrated many a time over. After all, the story recounted again, made the aged friends go down the memory lane; this made them relive the past. There is no gainsaying the fact, that the past is a prologue to life, for the past is the living sum of the present. "The past is an inspiration, for it drags us down and at the same time pushes us on," said Jawaharlal Nehru. Obviously, the past resuscitates, nay resurrects, the present.

Bhagwan vouchsafed that the one lesson he had learnt, though belatedly, was not to expose people when they were detected to be wrong in their utterings or depictions. For it was not enjoined on him to reform people, to make them perfect. Pointing out faults and characteristic infirmities in others, engendered squabbles and antagonism which invariably disturbed the peace of mind. "Resultantly, I have resolved to resort to blandishment instead of disparagement. Word of commendation, that is honey-words, are mood- enhancers, for me as also for others."

"Over the years, I have learnt not to bother about a spot on my shirt or trousers. It is personality, and not clothes, that speak louder than appearances. I shun people who do not value my words or my opinion. I remain cool when someone ridicules me, laughs, disdains, and trivializes me. I am convinced that I have no competition in the rat race, for I am not a rat. I am a thinking and pulsating human being, and above all, I am not in a race with anybody. As I grew older, I became mature and eventually learnt that I should not be embarrassed by my emotions. Owing to my emotions, I remain a pulsating human being. Besides, time has taught me to shun ego, because ego, by and large, begets and breeds rivalry, and enmity, among friends. Verily, ego may puff a man up, but it can never prop him up. And those who have ego eventually suffer owing to this malady."

Bhagwan *uvach:* "I live each day as if it is the last day. One who is born must die. Death acquits us of all obligations. Death shuts the gate of ego, envy, rivalry, acrimony, animosity. It is nature's way of telling us to slow down." My friend finally said that he was doing what made him happy; for it was he who was responsible for his joviality.

Verily, we should not look at old age as a burden, or as a decline. As long as breath lasts, man never retires. For man is of the earth, earthly. And as such he has all the minuses and pluses of the earth. There is no denying the fact that there are many wonderful things in nature, but the most wonderful of all is man. Man is a social animal. He is formed for society and is neither capable of living alone, nor has the courage to do it. And the mature averments of Bhagwan, my friend, substantiate this factum analysis, for the aged persons to emulate.

In fact, Bhagwan is nobody. He is only a persona, a character, a specimen, created to represent and speak for the aged people as to how they should conduct themselves when they grow old.

CHAPTER XXVI

What the Krishna Do We Mean?

Krishna is the god of many splendours. Varied and various are the aspects of his divinity. He is the incarnation of Lord Vishnu, the god of Preservation. He is the Krishna of the Mahabharata, a great strategist, pacifist and advisor. He is the Krishna of Kurukshetra, the great teacher, who manifested his Universal Form to his disciple Arjuna. He is the Krishna of the Gita, Song Celestial, a masterly discourse, an unrivalled philosophic-cum-religious thesis. He is the Krishna of Vrindavan, a god of love, in amorous dalliance with the gopis (cowherdesses). And he is the Christ of India, the saviour and redeemer of mankind.

Explaining the purpose of his birth, Krishna says in the Gita: "For the protection of the good, for the destruction of the wicked, and for the establishment of the righteousness, I come into being from age to age" (4.8). Krishna as incarnation of Vishnu is *'vyapke parameshvare'*: that is, having created the world, he afterwards entered into it. Vishnu is traced from the root 'vis,' that is to enter, to enter into Prakriti. In order to rid the world of the forces of evil, sin, ignorance, selfishness, and wicked oppressions, Lord Krishna descended to the earthly plane.

Krishna is from the root 'krish,' which means to scrape, because he scrapes, or draws away all sins and other sources of evil from his devotees. He who attracts all or arouses devotion in all is Krishna: *"karshati sarvam karshnah"*. Krishna is so-called because He removes the sins of his devotees. Krishna preached *loksangraha*, that is, universal brotherhood, *"sarva bhuta hite ratah:"* indulge yourself in the welfare of all creatures. Jung, the great psychologist opined: "In Christian countries, the Self is projected onto the second Adam, (that is) Christ. In the east, the relevant figure is that of Krishna." The fact remains that Krishna and Christ were the two manifestations of the same divinity separated by time and space.

Unlike Christ, who undertook to redeem mankind through his own sorrow and passion (His crucifixion), Krishna is the god of love and joy. He chose Vrindavan to celebrate his love-play (Ras Leela). When Krishna steals the clothes of the *gopis*, they request him to return them. "He exhorts them to come out because they must not conceal anything from their Lord. If they desired the boon of union with Krishna, if they professed that Krishna was the master of their inner souls, the Lord of their inner self, why should they conceal the outer form, the body from him?" They come out of the river, and receive their clothes, as also the divine grace.

When Krishna plays on his Flute in the woods. *Gopis* are so charmed that each one of them comes running, unmindful of their fathers, and husbands. They sing and dance with him. So intoxicated are they in love that they become oblivious of themselves. Each one of them feels that the Lord is dancing only with her, that she is the Lord's and the Lord is hers. It is One manifested in many: "*eko aham bahusyam.*" This is the cosmic form of Lord Krishna. The one Arjuna sees with his divine eye in the Gita.

This love-play between the "Divine cowherd" and the wives of the cowherds has nothing to do with the body, the physical presence. Their sinless souls achieved union with the Supreme without going through the process of yogic sadhana, or study of scriptures. The implied message in Ras Lila is that the devotees should learn to worship the Lord together and that none of them should ever want to own Him exclusively. The tenets of devotion demand: "Surrender, give, bestow, without claiming anything in return."

Krishna is divine, supreme, infinite Mind, Spirit, Soul, Principle, Life, Truth, Super Consciousness, Love, and a Unified God. This is the Krishna, whose name we chant with utmost reverence, deepest devotion, and feelings of love.

CHAPTER XXVII

Holy Waters: The Value of Tirtha

King Bhagirath did a long *tapasya* (penance) to bring the Ganga to this mortal world for the salvation of the souls of his dead ancestors. Pleased with the King's *tapasya*, the Ganga manifested to him. She promised to descend from heaven to earth, provided someone contained her mighty cascading flow. Bhagirath did more *tapasya*. Lord Shiva was propitiated. He absorbed the torrential flow of Ganga in his matted hair (jatayen). From thence flowed Ganga forever as a river on this earth. Immersed in the holy waters of the divine Ganga, the souls of Bhagirath's ancestors got salvation. This well-known mythical story that appears in the Bhagvat Purana gives significance to Haridwar as a *tirath* (a place of pilgrimage). Down the ages, we have been seeking salvation for the souls of our dead kin by immersing their ashes in the sacred waters of the Ganga.

Thus, the journey to a *tirath* becomes an archetypal symbol. The concept of man as a pilgrim, and of life as a pilgrimage, is common to a great many peoples and traditions. Holy scriptures postulate that man comes to this world as a pilgrim and goes to his original home after completing the allotted journey. This connotation of life as a journey lends pilgrimage its value.

The root of the word *tirath* is 'tri' with the suffix 'th' added to it. "Tri" stands for 'tir', that is, the bank of a river. Therefore, it means to cross over the "bhavsagar" of unrighteousness, of trials and tribulations, as also to swim across the river of ignorance to the realm of knowledge. The suffix 'th' connotes 'pavitramahi', that is 'piety' or 'sanctity.' After a visit to a "tirath", or for that matter a dip in the holy waters there, for example in the rivers Ganga, or the Yamuna, a pilgrim is sanctified with piety and godly grace. By implications, holy waters cleanse a man of all sins, dirt and dross. He experiences a renewal of life.

Tiraths, by and large, are situated on the banks of the rivers, or the lakes. The Vedas propound that water is the main source of fertility. It is symbolic of spiritual awakening and existential revitalization. Pilgrims return home with containers full of 'water of salvation' of the Ganga and many other rivers. Water sustains human life. And so does a *tirath* which sustains our faith in the omniscient, omnipotent God.

"Tri" also means three. According to the ancient scriptures, there are four 'essentials', for a man to realize in this world. They are *dharam* (righteousness), *arth* (wealth) *kam* (desire) and *moksha* (deliverance). Of the four *arth*, that is money, a pilgrim has and spends on the pilgrimage. Without money, no pilgrimage can be undertaken. It is for the achievement of the remaining three -- *dharam, kam and moksha* – that one undertakes an arduous journey to a place of pilgrimage.

From time immemorial, sacred rivers, holy shrines, and abodes of gods have beckoned us. But of late, spiritual channels on the TV, have promoted religious tourism. And as such religious tourism is fast getting precedence over pilgrimages, blurring the distinction between a pilgrim and a tourist.

CHAPTER XXVIII

Morsel of Human Love

Jagdish, a shrewd businessman, opened a showroom in the busy market of his town. He stocked therein ready-made garments of the latest fashion and design, both for men and women. And in order to run his business smoothly and efficiently, he had engaged four hands, two men and two women, all young and in their late twenties. They were paid Rs 12,000 each as salary per month. They attended to the customers, mostly ladies, and showed them all kinds of garments. Soon the business proliferated, and the dame luck smiled on him.

It was the best of times for Jagdish. His business venture flourished and he earned enough and to spare. But eventually, his destiny took a turn for the worse. In the closest vicinity of his showroom came up a mega mall which besides other things, also sold all sorts of garments. Resultantly, his business dwindled. His daily earnings were reduced to less than half as compared to his income earlier. So, he reluctantly thought to reduce the strength of his employees one by one. In fact, so kind-hearted and humane was Jagdish that he did not want to remove any of his workers as that would have meant penury for the poor employees. He felt bad for his decision. But he was helpless. There was no alternative except to cut the expenses on account of the wages.

His decision to dispense with the service of one of his employees, so unnerved him that he could not sleep throughout the night. He suffered from a sleep disorder; and continued to toss on the bed from one side to another. Nevertheless, the next day when he left for the showroom, he was, literally crestfallen and melancholy. As he sauntered towards his showroom, he continued to ruminate over the matter as who among the four workers should be the first to be dismissed from service. He felt that he could not turn out any of the two women as that would badly affect whatever little business was left. For, those two young and smart girls showed the garments to the women-customers, used their persuasive manners and lured them to buy clothes. It was owing to these two girls that garments, by and large, were sold.

As regards the two men, he was flabbergasted a bit because both of them hailed from poor families One of them was an old employee who worked with Jagdish for more than six years. And the other was the only earning member of the family. Nevertheless, he decided not to remove the senior worker, but the junior one, a fresher named Kundan. He resolved within himself that Kundan should go. Jagdish reasoned out that Kundan would not suffer the pangs of poverty since his brother worked in a factory, and got a hefty salary sufficient to make both ends meet. Besides, Kundan, being quite sharp, good-natured and always smiling, would get a job elsewhere. "Since I am completely dissipated financially, I will have to remove one of the workers, and in the first instance he would be Kundan."

Jagdish pondered over the difficult situation en route to his showroom. When he reached there depressed and dejected, he called his workers and in a patronising tone spoke to them: "You know the financial position of the showroom as presently obtained. The business has shrunk a great deal, and as such the showroom has virtually become a petty shop. Therefore, I can no longer afford to keep all four of you in employment. One of you will have to leave the job." Jagdish's throat choked when he made this announcement. In order to wet his throat a little, he drank water from a bottle. He declared: "Kundan! You need not come on duty from tomorrow. I know it is an unpleasant and unsavoury decision, but I am helpless. However, young and good-natured as you are, you will be able to find a job elsewhere. Moreover, your brother is also in a job. He earns well to sustain the family. There is no immediacy in finding work. You will get some job soon enough." Kundan felt, literally knocked down. His face changed colour; it suddenly turned pale. The other colleagues (Sohan, Urvashi and Jyoti) too felt despondent, dispirited and uncomfortable. One of the two girls, named Jyoti, who lived in the close vicinity of Kundan, felt disheartened and gloomy. She fumbled a bit in a bid to say something. Jagdish, a humane person as he was, understood that she wanted to say something. He asked her; "Daughter, I think you want to say something. Speak out your mind sans any hesitation." Jyoti said in a condescending tone: "Uncle, Kundan's brother is also not doing anything these days. He is idle. He lost his job a fortnight ago. Besides, Kundan's mother is ill. He has to take care of her treatment and health."

Jagdish then looked at the depressed demeanour of Kundan and felt aghast to find tears wallowing in the eyes of his young worker. These were the tears of responsibility, of his filial concern for his ailing mother. These were the tears of worry for his brother, now out of avocation. He tried to hide his ever-beaming grin on his visage. Nevertheless, before Jagdish could utter a word, Urvashi, seemingly a mature girl, propounded: "Jagdish uncle, if you don't mind, may I give you a suggestion to overcome the present quandary." Jagdish said; "Please speak out your mind." Urvashi submitted: "Uncle! You need not remove anybody from the service. Instead, reduce the emoluments of all of us to the extent of saving the salary of Kundan. You pay a monthly salary of Rupees 12,000 to each one of us. You decrease it by 3000 and pay a salary of Rupees 9000 each. In this way, you will salvage Rupees 12,000 a month, equal to the wages of Kundan." Both Jyoti and Sohan, the other two, too agreed to this proposal. They accepted the cut in the wages to save the job of Kundan.

They said: "Yes uncle! We agree to the proposal. We will make do with a lesser salary of Rupees 9000 each, instead of Rupees 12,000 a month. Let it be our yeoman's service to rescue Kundan from penury and destitution." Jagdish felt relieved. The burden on his heart was lifted. His problem was solved. He was out of the quagmire; thanks to the suggestion of Urvashi. He uttered a sigh of relief. Then he asked: "I hope the cut in the monthly wages of each of you, will not be detrimental to your sustenance. And all of you will be able to make do with lesser emoluments." The foursome said in unison: "We agreed to the salary cut on our own volition. There is no question of any regret. Owing to this decision, none of us will suffer the pangs of deprivation and hunger. Instead of leading a life of impoverishment, it is better to reduce our morsels to some extent."

The goodwill gesture of the four young wage-earners, perforce brought tears into the eyes of Jagdish. These were tears of satisfaction, of joy. Following this colloquy, all the four workers engaged themselves in their daily work. "Verily, they turned out to be bigger in stature and thinking than me," thought Jagdish.

The story has a salubrious moral. All of us should help those who need support, finance and morals. Let nobody go hungry. One should eat to live, and not live to eat. "I was hungered, and ye gave me food. I was thirsty, and ye gave me water. I was a stranger, and ye took me in. Naked, and you clothed me. I was sick, and ye visited me," propounded Lord Christ in the Bible. Obviously, one who gives is more blessed than one who receives. The living need charity more than the dead.

CHAPTER XXIX

The Dweller and the Dwelling

Bhola after a very long time went to the residential colony where he had lived for many years before going abroad in search of greener pastures. He was surprised to see the complete metamorphosis in the infrastructure and the living ambience. Many new houses had come up. There were multistorey buildings. Nothing appeared to be familiar. Most of the faces roaming hither and thither were unfamiliar. The entire scenario in the colony had undergone a complete transformation. Nonetheless, he undertook a tour of the colony, located his old friends and neighbours, and had affectionate interaction and intimate conversation. Just then he espied an old familiar face. He walked up to him. The man was accoutred in a blue uniform. He obviously appeared to be a guard employed on the security duty by the colony dwellers. As soon as the guard saw Bhola, he sauntered apace, folded his hands and touched his feet. Then he said: "Sir! Pranam." Though Bhola recognized his countenance, he could not recall his name. The guard fathomed the discomfiture of Bhola. Then he averred: "Bhola sir! I hope you have not recognised me. I am Babu. I worked in the house of Maya Aunty, your erstwhile neighbour."

Bhola peeped into the memory lane and remembered Babu. "Babu! You have become quite healthy. Earlier you were thin and lean. But now you have gained a lot of weight. How is Maya Aunty?" Babu smiled. He said that she had gone. "Where?" Bhola asked. "Her son was in America. She affectionately called him Sonu. She must have gone to America to live with Sonu. She did well. How could she live alone in old age in such a spacious house?" Hearing these words, Babu became silent. Then with all seriousness and a sad face, he said: "Sir! She has gone to God." "When did she die?" asked Bhola. "About six months ago," Babu replied. Bhola again enquired; "What did she die of? What happened to her?"

Babu replied: "Nothing happened to her, she died of old age. Old age is a disease in itself. Her son had also not come for many years. She always talked of him. She longed to see Sonu before she breathed her last. But it did not happen. Her yearning to meet her son gnawed into her mind, always muttering something unintelligible." Bhola again asked: "Why did she not go to her son?" Bhola philosophically propounded: "It was the usual worry of all aged parents living alone. She did not want to leave her house and go to America to be with her son. I invariably suggested to her to go abroad and spend the rest of her life with her son. But she always reasoned out that she had built her house with great difficulty and care, and she did not want someone to usurp it in her absence."

Said Bhola: "Yes! I know that. In the absence of the house-owner, anyone can occupy, nay seize, the house property, especially when the owner is aged and living abroad. However, I admire your characteristic idiosyncrasies. You served Maya Aunty with all care and devotion. Since she is no more, what do you do now?" Babu smiled again, and said: "what can I do? Earlier, I was alone. Now I have brought my family from the village. My wife along with my two children live with me here in the house left behind by Maya Aunty." Babu further pointed out: "After the death of Aunty, her son came, and stayed here for a week. Before leaving, he told me to look after the house in his absence. "I know it is a big house with four spacious rooms and a sprawling lawn. How could I live in such a huge house alone? So, I brought my family. Moreover, it was enjoined on me to look after the maintenance of the house. He has been sending a handsome amount every month to meet the routine expenses on the upkeep of the house. Eventually, the colony-walas engaged me as a chowkidar. In the meanwhile, I got my children admitted to the nearby school. I am now living here in this house with ease. Sonu left all household goods – fridge, TV, beds, sofa, a cycle, for me to use. For he could not take all these articles to America."

The turn of events surprised and confused Bhola. Babu earlier used the cycle as his mode of conveyance when Maya was alive.

He did all the domestic errands, such as going to the market to fetch things of daily need, on cycle. Now Babu plied a motorcycle. Sonu "handed over" the house to Babu in the hope that he would look after the house-property meticulously and ensure its proper maintenance and upkeep. Besides the house would escape being forcibly occupied by land-mafia.

Bhola ruminated over the factum situation and eventually felt that building a house was an arduous proposition, highly expensive and cumbersome. He convinced himself that Maya Aunty did not go to live with her son, lest somebody should occupy her house in her absence. And furthermore, Sonu handed over the house to Babu to live in it and upkeep and maintain it in his absence. "Verily, Maya and Sonu are not only the chowkidars (watchmen) of their houses but perhaps all other house owners too are the "watchdogs" of the residences built by them.

Bhola finally asked:"Did you tell Sonu that you have brought your family to live with you in the house, of which you are just the keeper, the caretaker?" Babu said nonchalantly: "What is there to be told to Sonu? He is not likely to come here from that afar in America. And what would he do alone, if he decides to return to live in this house? Keeping this fact in mind, I brought my family. If ever he comes, I will see what can or should be done. When His mother was alive, he did not care to visit her mother. I don't think he would ever return following the death of his mother. And then, why should he bother about the house? I am here to look after it; I am not going to supplant it, uproot it, and take it away to my village. I am only guarding the house-property, so that it may not fall into unscrupulous hands." After having said this, Babu smiled. This time it was not his usual smile, but a Machiavellian smile, a smile of a scoundrel, of one expert in hoodwinking.

Bhola was aghast to meet and have a colloquy with Babu. He muttered to himself: "Maya Aunty who had built the house for her progeny, eventually was transmuted into a "tavern," to be grabbed by someone dishonest, a crook." He concluded that Bhola was no longer an erstwhile minion of Maya Aunty, but had now virtually become a house-owner. The dweller usurped the dwelling. Sonu would never reclaim his house again.

Crestfallen and introspective, Bhola said goodbye and left Babu. He had walked a few steps when he turned back and propounded: "Babu! Wise people say that only fools build houses, while worldly-wise men occupy and live in them." Babu soon reacted to what Bhola had said: "Sir! It is the handiwork of luck, for fortune favours the brave." Bhola spoke to himself: "Not brave, but usurpers, tricksters."

Bhola walked away thinking "It is really the handiwork of fate." At his back, Babu had a hearty laugh, which pierced Babu's ears like the horse laugh of a rogue. The words of Babu echoed: "I am not going to take the house. I am only looking after it." These words banged, literally clobbered, the conscience of Bhola. Traversing the distance fast, he ruminated: "Nobody takes the house with him. So long as he lives, he only looks after it. How true is the dictum! This is true of all of us. One does not know when the messengers of Death will come to take the breath away. So long as we are breathing, we should live happily. And follow what Lord Krishna said in the Gita: "*loksamgraha*," universal brotherhood, coming together of all people, that is the interconnectedness of society."

CHAPTER XXX

The Power of Guru Mantra

There lived a thief in a town. He broke into the houses of all kinds of people, rich and not-so-rich, affluent and middle-class denizens, in the nocturnal darkness, and stole whatever he could lay his hands on. But in order to hoodwink the people and escape being caught, he followed a subterfuge of being a devotee of a hermit and visited his hermitage almost daily. He would join the congregation and listen to the spiritual discourse delivered by the saint. He also performed different errands, such as sweeping and cleaning the ashram, milking the cows, serving and feeding the inmates of the hermitage. Eventually, the hermit was so impressed by the devotion and dedication of the thief that he wanted to make him his disciple. So, one day the saint, popularly called Guruji, called him and told him that in view of his commitment to religious tenets, he had decided to anoint him as his disciple. The Guru gave him the Guru-mantra and directed him to lead a pious life and follow a path of truth and righteousness.

However, the thief felt a little edgy, apprehensive, and flustered. For many days he pondered over the matter. At last, he finally resolved to tell Guruji the truth as to who he was. He approached the Guruji in his hut, touched his feet, and said: "Guruji, I am a thief. As you know bad habits die hard. It would be well-nigh impossible for me to abandon thievery. Therefore, the guru-mantra to follow good and honest human conduct, would be an arduous proposition for me." Nevertheless, the Guru said: "Don't bother about what you are. I give you another mantra to live up to in life." "Guruji! What is that alternative mantra I need to adhere to." The Guru said that, "the backup mantra is that you would consider all women, except your wife, as your mothers and sisters, and care for them with filial affection." The thief promised to follow the guru-mantra, nay the diktat, of his Guru.

One day, in the night, he left the ashram incognito and travelled to the neighbouring state to apprise himself of the populace and their idiosyncrasies there. When he reached the neighbouring state, he found that the king had abandoned his queen and housed her in an old castle outside the urban boundaries. The fault of the queen was that she was sterile, barren, and did not give birth to an heir to succeed the king on the throne. So, she was deserted, nay discarded, in the virtually "haunted" castle to live alone. The "haunted house" was well guarded by a big contingent of soldiers.

One day, something unusual happened. The thief broke into the castle in a bid to commit burglary. Hearing the noise, the queen woke up. She espied the burglar. But she did not raise any alarm; nor did she alert the sentries on duty to apprehend the thief. Since she lived a life of loneliness, she always longed to have the company of someone to talk to. For, a human being is a social animal. He or she always needs the company of fellow beings to interact and converse with. There is no gainsaying the fact that the loneliness is such a gnawing malady that debilitates and destroys the loner. On the other hand, the sentries on duty dared not enter the bed chamber of the queen as they afeared the unforeseen back-lash. Therefore, they decided to apprise the king that a person of unknown credentials had entered the queen's chamber clandestinely and that she seemed to be quite friendly with him. So much so that they exaggerated the happening to the extent that the queen seemed to have intimate relations with the stranger.

The king told his minions that they should hush up the matter, lest the common people should have an inkling of it. He would himself covertly see the conduct and behaviour of the queen. The king sneaked into the castle surreptitiously. What he saw and overheard, was an eye-opener for him. The queen asked the stranger: "How have you come, and on what mode of conveyance?" The thief replied: "Lady! I came on a camel. And with the help of the howdah on the camel's back, I climbed the castle wall, and entered into your chamber."

The queen, then, proposed: "I will fill the howdah with gold and diamonds if you fulfil my desire." The thief remembered the mantra of his hermit-guru. He averred: "Respected lady, you are like my mother. In fact, you very much resemble my mother. If you have any errands, please tell me, your son, sans any hesitation. I would do whatever you enjoin me to do. To fulfil any other desire, except the mother's desire, would virtually be a loathsome act in contravention of the guru-mantra." When the king overheard the conversation, he said to himself: "What a quaint chance to witness a strange colloquy! A thief and so honest a human being!"

The king ordered the soldier to arrest the stranger and bring him to his palace. When the thief appeared, the king said patronisingly: "I am highly pleased with your honesty and ethical morality. Ask for any reward that you want!" The thief extracted a promise from the king that he would grant him what he desired. Then he solicited: "Rajan, my mother, the queen, whom you have abandoned and discarded to live alone in a dilapidated castle, adopt her as your legitimate spouse, and restore her to her royal status of a queen." This made the king extremely happy. He had the feelings of salubrious glee. Ever since the king had deserted his wife as a sterile, barren woman, it was for the first time the king experienced a sense of solace. In fact, it was a moment of rectitude. He wanted to make amends for his erroneous and fallacious conduct. So, he commanded that the queen be immediately brought from the old crumbling castle and that she should be embellished in the royal robes, and brought to the palace with all the fanfare and honour. As soon as the queen appeared, the king got up from his seat, walked up to his spouse, and hugged her affectionately. Then the king pleaded: "Royal lady, I have caused you a lot of pain and agony. I am guilty of unscrupulous and unrighteous acts. Please forgive me for my delinquency and misdemeanour. In order to make amends for my blunder and folly, I want to expiate for my sin. Therefore, I not only supplicate that I may be pardoned but also request you to demand anything you wish as a recompense." The queen said: "Please put your commitment on a paper with the royal stamp affixed to it so that you would grant what I demand." The king agreed and did what the queen supplicated.

The queen said: "Rajan! We do not have any progeny. Therefore, adopt this thief as your son. Since he calls me his mother, I must fulfil the motherly obligation. Please anoint him as your heir apparent." The king said: "*Tathastu*!" Be it so. Verily, one guru-mantra of a sage turned a thief into a king. So much power the words of the saints carry. Time to follow and remember this dictum!

CHAPTER XXXI

Ursula: The German Friend

During my world trotting, I scoured varied countries of men and manners. There were two unique happenings which were indelibly instilled in my mind. I often recall them and cherish their memory.

It so happened that on the first leg of my world tour, I planned to visit Scandinavian countries. I rang up Onkar Singh, a close friend, who migrated from Jullundur in Punjab to Oslo (the capital of Norway), and had settled there, where he ran a famous Pizza hut. When I informed him about my trip to Oslo, he requested me to bring "sugar cane, a few bottles of Old Monk rum, and Namkeen of various types from Haldi Ram." The wish-list surprised me a bit. I was rather flabbergasted, as to why he needed Old Monk Rum while there was no dearth of Scotch Whisky in his country. Nonetheless, I procured sugar cane from the Okhla Market, cut it into two-feet-long pieces, and neatly tied them in a bundle. Similarly, I procured four bottles of Old Monk Rum. I concealed the sugar cane pieces, and the Rum bottles in my portmanteau.

When I reached Oslo, Onkar was there at the airport to receive me. It was the first week of May. While in Delhi, people were afflicted by the buffets of intense heat-wave, in Oslo the weather was congenial and soothing. As soon as I reached his home, I opened my bags, took out the sugar cane pieces, Rum bottles and Namkeen, and gave them to Onkar. After having relaxed for a couple of hours to undo the jet- lag, I settled with Onkar on the small lush green lawn outside his newly built house. There were gathered about half-a-dozen friends, all hailing from different towns of Punjab. In fact, Oslo has a large population of Indians, mostly Punjabis.

To my astonishment, Onkar gave each one of them one piece of sugar cane. This unique gift from an Indian friend engendered a winsome smile of joy on their faces; they appeared to be mighty pleased because for them it was the most precious and cherished gift. The reasons as to why the gift was so valuable and gratifying, were not far to seek. Firstly, they came from their homeland. And secondly, it epitomized the Punjabi culture and gusto. And thirdly, it invoked the "Indianness" embedded in their hearts and minds. That is why a sign of contentment, nay glee, was writ large on their brows. All of them thanked me in unison for the gift.

Besides, there was another surprise for me. After the sugar cane "ceremony," all of us sat down for a drinking session. Onkar opened Old Monk and served that "desi sharab" to his friends and himself. And for me, he opened Blue Label Scotch whisky. Onkar and his friends relished Old Monk since it represented India, the Indian idiosyncrasies, nay the *punjabiat* of Punjab.

And yet there was another surprise for me. The drinking bout continued till late in the night. It was beyond midnight, according to the Indian Standard Time. But in Oslo, it was still daylight. The sun shone as bright as 12 noon in the day. When I asked about this natural phenomenon, Onkar told me that Norway was the land of the perennial sun. "The sun sets here only for a couple of hours, and that too in the wee hours. When the sun supposedly sets, there is no complete darkness, but just the twilight." I was amazed. In fact, it was a surfeit of wonder.

While staying in Oslo, Onkar took me to Denmark as also to Sweden. After staying in the Scandinavian countries for nine days, I repaired to London. In London, there was nothing new which I did not know. So, within four days I embarked on the second leg of my tour to Europe.

I boarded the Euro-rail and reached Paris in the afternoon. In Paris, I had decided to go to Venice, and from there to Rome, and then visit other places, including New York and Canada. While I was standing in the queue to book a seat in the Euro-rail for Venice, I received a call from Kuldeep on my cell phone from Bremen, a famous shipping town in Germany. Kuldeep and I had been close friends from our college days. After graduation, he had shifted to Bremen, where he worked in a ship-manufacturing unit.

Kuldeep asked me: "What is your tour schedule? Why don't you come to Bremen, a bustling shipping town with many places of tourist attraction?" I told him: "I am heading towards Venice. And from there I would go to Rome. On my way back, I will visit Bremen." But Kuldeep insisted that "You should first visit Bremen, and from there you could go to Venice and Rome." He persisted and asserted that he would be off duty tomorrow and the day after, being Saturday and Sunday. And as such he would have two free days "to take me round the town, to the water bodies, and other places."

I could not say "no" to his suggestion. So, I booked a berth for Bremen. The train reached Bremen the next morning, just a little before sunrise. I alighted from the train and came out of the station. There had been heavy rain in Bremen the previous night. Therefore, the weather was chilly. A cold wave was blowing. Standing on the road outside the Station, I felt freezing cold; my body shivered in the petrifying icy wind. I needed a cup of coffee. But I did not have the Deutsche Mark, the German currency. I sauntered back to the Railway Station. There I saw an official sitting behind a window. I approached him to seek his help: "Sir! I am a tourist from India. I want to get a traveller's cheque exchanged with the German currency. Can you guide me to the money changer?" The official did not know much English. Whatever little I could make out of his "tooti-phooti" (broken) English, he appeared to have told me: "The Money Changer will be available after 10 AM." He then indicated towards a hotel across the road and advised me to go there. "The staff on duty in the hotel, well versed in English, might help to solve my predicament," he said.

Accordingly, I crossed the road and reached the hotel. As soon as I entered the hotel, I felt some relief from the bitter cold. A young lady was there on the counter. I immediately walked up to her: "Good morning, Madam! I am a tourist from India. I am confronted with a dilemma. Firstly, I need a cup of coffee to warm myself up in this chilly weather. Secondly, I do not have Deutsche Mark, though I have the traveller's cheque. I am told that the Money Changer would be available after 10 AM. Thirdly, I want to ring up my friend to inform him that I have arrived and that he should come to fetch me." The lady gave me a winsome smile, as bewitching as her countenance and demeanour looked to be. She immediately took out a 20- Deutsche Mark note from her purse and gave it to me. She said: "There is a market close by. You can have coffee and some snacks there. Meanwhile, please give me the number of your friend. I will ring him up and inform him about your arrival, and request him to escort you home."

It was a highly benevolent gesture. That German lady was obviously a personification of beatitude. As guided by her, I went to the coffee shop and had a hot cup of coffee with a cheese sandwich. In the meanwhile, the sun had arisen. The cold wave had abated a little. I slowly returned to the hotel. There my friend was present and waiting for me. I shook hands with him and narrated him the entire episode. I also informed him that the gentle lady at the counter had loaned him 20 Deutsche Mark. So, I requested Kuldeep to refund the money to the lady, plus the telephone charges for ringing him up. Kuldeep took out the money from his pocket to give it to the lady. But she would not take the money. I repeatedly insisted and persisted, but she said "No." When I asked her as to why she was not accepting the money, she averred: "You are from India. India is a friendly nation. We have cultural and historical relations with your great country. Sanskrit and German are sister-languages. Sanskrit is very popular in Germany. And so are the Indian scriptures, the Vedas, the Upanishads, the Gita, etc. There have been very many scholars, even scientists, who were very well-read in Sanskrit. Therefore, from an Indian friend, I will not accept the money. Let it be a friendly gesture from a German to an Indian friend."

What she did and said made me emotional. I liked the humane human being in her. Both my friend and I profusely thanked her. Being gratified by her friendly and philanthropic nature, I asked her name. She said: "My name is Ursula." After that, I boarded the car of Kuldeep and left for his two-room apartment.

Kuldeep booked a berth in the Sunday evening Euro-rail for Venice. Before boarding the train, I walked into the hotel and met Ursula again to say goodbye to her. She gave me an affectionate hug and took my address and phone number. She also gave me her phone number and address.

When I returned to India, a month later, after visiting America and Canada, one day in the morning I got a call from Ursula. We exchanged greetings and had a heart-to-heart colloquy. Since then, Ursula and I have been in regular touch. Several years after this friendship, my granddaughter went to Germany to do M.Sc., and Ph.D. in Micro Biology. Ursula looked after her like her mother. Verily, a holy passion of friendship accentuates into sweet and steady fondness, nay affection and rapport, that lasts a whole lifetime.

CHAPTER XXXII

PM–PHOBIA: A political malady

A big-bellied fat person, accoutred in white khadi Kurta and pyjama with a matching jacket, lies supine on a bed. This leviathan of a person, weighing about 120 KG, is a veteran politician. His name is Satyarthi, but in the local parlance, he is referred to as Netaji. His name may be Satyarthi, but his karmas are quite antithetical to what is implied in his nomenclature. Lying on the bed, he appears to be quite uncomfortable bellowing intermittently suppressed babel of pain. Owing to uneasy sleep, he is rolling on the bed from one side to another and vice-versa. His wife, Savitri, a caressing and devoted better-half, enters his room with a desi concoction of some pain-relieving medicine and affectionately tells him to sip it. Netaji, like an obedient boy, drinks the Ayurvedic medicine. But it has no effect. His belly-ache does not subside. Savitri is flabbergasted to see the condition of her husband.

The political career of Netaji extends over more than two decades. During such a protracted politicking, he contested and won several elections, became MLA and MP and recently a Minister too. But he lost the last election, lock, stock and barrel, because the electorates, who had returned him to the state legislature and Lok Sabha repeatedly, forfeited their faith, nay hope, in him. Being idle sans any political status, he has become disoriented, and his appetite and sleep have gone awry. The after-effect of this political neglect, this spurn by the populace, made him sick. And now he is suffering from the *pait dard* (stomach-ache).

Outside his room sit his political Secretaries, Mange Ram and Dhani Ram. The common people of the constituency of Netaji, in obvious antipathy, refer to them as "Demanding Ram," and "Money Ram." For they were the agents of Netaji. On behalf of their leader in power, they brazenly pilfered and purloined the government coffers and the helpless common populace. With anxiety writ large on their faces, they appeared to be distracted and worried, for their future, qua the pecuniary advantages, were linked with the power and pelf of Netaji. They retained ten percent of the dirty lucre they collected for their leader. With Netaji's hangers-on was sitting a swarm of Netaji's supporters.

Over the years, instead of being a popular political leader, Satyarthi turned out to be "a dealer in hope." He is not what he used to be. The words of Mark Twain, the famous American novelist: "leader is the most rapscallion," that is, rascal, never-do-well person, convincingly apply to Satyarthi. Instead of submerging himself into the fountain of the plebians, he only floated in the moat of self-importance. The populace never likes a conceited, big-headed leader. The loss of confidence of the general public is one of the reasons for his *pait dard* (belly-ache).

Mange Ram, that is Demanding Ram, and Dhani Ram, qua Money Ram, deliberated with the crowd of hangers-on, the reasons for the illness of Netaji. Eventually, the discussion veered around to the point of ameliorating the lot of the Netaji, vis-s-vis his physical ailment. They desired and aspired to make all-out efforts to help Netaji regain his earlier status and position of pre-eminence. However, Mange Ram averred that the cause of Netaji's affliction was something else. Ever since Satyarthi Ji returned from the political conclave, he has been unwell. Neither does he eat well, nor can he sleep well. His malady is getting aggravated with every passing day.

But before the real cause of his affliction could be addressed, it was imperative to cure him of the disease he presently suffered from. So, it was suggested that they must request Savitri Madam to call in the doctor to provide the medical treatment. Any further delay would be detrimental to Netaji. Accordingly, Savitri rang up Dr Daya Shankar, a family physician, to come post haste. The doctor arrived within minutes with his medical kit. He thoroughly checked Netaji, examined his pulse, and took his blood pressure. Everything seemed to be normal. Daya Shankar failed to identify the cause of *pait dard.* He asked Mange Ram: "What did Satyarthi eat last night?" Mange Ram replied: "He ate a roasted chicken, a bowl of fried fish, and two plates of mutton Biryani. He also took four pegs of whisky as a digestive." The doctor asked yet another question: "Is this his normal diet?" "No," said Mange Ram. "After he returned from the meeting of the political leaders of regional and family parties, his hunger shrank a great deal. As MLA, MP and later as Union Minister, he was such a voracious eater that he gobbled acres of farmers' land, and gorged Sarkari and gair- sarkari (Government and non-government) landed property. His ever-hungry stomach consumed many bridges, schools, public-oriented welfare infrastructure, and development schemes. After having eaten so much, *kabhi dakar tak nahi liya* (he never eructated, that is belched). But now he does not have the "rich fare," he earlier acquired to satiate his hunger.

This made Doctor Daya Shankar pensive. He pondered over the difficult medical case. He took out the stethoscope, hung it on his ears, and checked his heartbeat. Then he groped his stomach. But he did not find any ailment. The functioning of all the major parameters was smooth sans any debility, fault and frailty. The doctor, then, asked Satyarthi Ji, to show his tongue. When Netaji opened his mouth and stretched his tongue out, the inside of his mouth, teeth and tongue, were horribly besmeared with red colour of the beetle and tobacco which Satyarthi chewed.

Dr Daya Shankar thought of knowing more about the patient. He requested Mange Ram to tell him the case history, for he was not in a position to ascertain the ailment and the cause of it. Mange Ram, being the all-weather aid of Netaji, knew everything about his leader, as he always stood by him through thick and thin. He said: "Satyarthi Ji is woe begone owing to something serious, fatuous and inane." The doctor was surprised a little to hear this. He became inquisitive to know more, and asked "What is that? These days he suffers from PM-PHOBIA. The doctor asked: "Is it some new epidemic? I have never heard of this disease before." Mange Ram averred: "Yes! It is a disease worse than any epidemic hitherto known. These days this chronic affliction has caught many a politician, especially the regional and family political outfits."

Mange Ram further posited: "His friends and well-wishers deposited in his mind that he had been MLA and MP several times. Therefore, as a veteran political leader, he has the acumen to become the Prime Minister. And given his renown and reputation, he was suitably qualified to be declared as the PM candidate in the ensuing election to the Parliament. Therefore, this notion, nay this hope, so inculcated into his inflated ego, and implanted on the tablet of his psyche, could be the mainspring of his mental and physical agony, and the consequential dwindling of appetite and sleep. For uneasy lies the head that wears the crown," opined Mange Ram.

Just then, Dhani Ram, the other sycophant of Netaji, interjected: "Obviously, the cause of illness appertains to Satyarthi's burning desire to become the PM. And as such, the epidemic called PM-phobia, which has caught many politicians these days, emanates out of this malaise." Mange Ram nodded his head in agreement. He added that owing to the failed aspiration, Netaji suffered cramps. Often the spasmodic spasms engendered a fit of delirium, and the resultant pait dard (belly-ache).

At this point, Savitri propounded: "There is no denying the fact that the politicians, while in power, hardly fall sick. Rather their health improves. But when they lose power, and their political prestige, qua eminence, is pruned and downsized, then "somebody" becomes "nobody." Following the defeat at the hustings, Satyarthi had to vacate the official accommodation. And all other perks which accompany an elected person were also snatched. So, he lamented the loss of political power. Left with no alternative, he shifted with his bag and baggage to a smaller house. Such commingling of detrimental and hostile happenings accentuated his depression, his anguish."

Nonetheless, Netaji was a political creature made of different woof and warp. The loss of the election, of ministership, of power and pelf, made him more aggressive. He was itching to regain what he had lost. The aspirations aroused by his flatterers that he was the fittest material to become the Prime Minister, activated him, nay literally animated and actuated him. Satyarthi was not the person to be thwarted by defeat for long. He galvanised his resources, contacted his friends in varied regional political outfits, and "family parties," and convinced them that they should all come together, form a political alliance, and nominate one candidate for the post of the Prime Ministership in the next election. Eventually, several political leaders, who were sulking owing to the many cases of corruption and money-laundering, registered by anti-corruption agencies (ED, CBI, etc), resolved to form a political alliance to supplant the present Prime Minister with a person of their collective choice. And if they succeed in their mission, they would escape various enquiries and court cases. Accordingly, leaders of various political parties, most of them guilty of corruption and on bail, decided to hold a conclave to deliberate on the political situation and nominate, or select, one candidate for the post of the Prime Minister. The first meeting of about 15 political parties was held in the capital of an eastern state. The entire expenditure was borne by the Chief Minister of that state. Netaji Satyarthi was the most vocal at the conclave.

In his inspired and inspiring speech, he postulated: "Friends and countrymen! We are passing through the worst of times. We have to collectively stand up against the menace perpetrated by the present government. Union is strength. If we act in unison, we are bound to succeed. Let us nominate here and now an able, experienced and popular Neta, like the one I am, as the candidate for the Prime Ministership in the coming elections."

Reacting to the political diatribe of Satyarthi, Jagdish Babu, the leader of a regional outfit, in his hissing voice, pointed out: "The selection of a candidate for the coveted post of the Prime Ministership, requires prolonged and in-depth deliberations. Why only Satyarthi? There are many other leaders present here, who are equally capable and experienced, and most deserving to ascend to the top post. So, let us not be in a hurry." Subscribing to the suggestion of Jagdish Babu, Sharda Pawarlekar another regional leader, said: "Such a momentous decision cannot be taken in in hurry and scurry. Let us enjoy the sumptuous fare arranged by our host." All the other Netas attending the conclave proposed that they should meet again after a month. In the meantime, all the leaders, collectively or individually, should do homework and come up with tangible proposals to ruminate over.

The Leaders dispersed sans any decision. However, it was decided to meet again, after a month, in the capital of a southern state. Since the conclave turned out to be a nullity, Satyarthi was highly disappointed, nay disgusted, that nobody paid any heed to his hypothesis. Obviously, his hope to become the PM candidate, was dashed. Nevertheless, he thought that he would try his luck again at the next meeting of the conclave. On the stipulated date, he reached there. What happened was disappointing. There was, literally a "quarrelsome" exchange of hot words between leaders of various parties. Netas vied with each other to become the Prime Minister. Verily, each one of them suffered from PM-phobia. When it appeared that the meeting would turn out to be a negation of purpose, an enthusiastic communicator of a political party, snatched the mike and started speaking. His name was Hello Ram. He said: "Since it appears that there are several leaders aspiring to become the Prime Minister, I propose that each Chief Minister be elevated as Prime Minister of the state he rules."

Sharda Pawarlekar: "How can that be possible? There has to be only one Prime Minister to rule the country. The country cannot have twenty Prime Ministers as proposed by Hello Ram. The world will laugh at us." In the meantime, Rani Romana, a cunning and astute female leader, literally snatched the mike from the hands of Sharda and announced: "Don't bother about what the world will think. There is a positive logic in the suggestion of my aid, Hello Ram. There is a precedent before us. Not in the distant past, the state of Jammu and Kashmir had a Prime Minster. Therefore, the example is before us. We can follow the Kashmir prototype, of course with modifications."

Then rose Mehul Wangchuk, a young and aspiring leader. He said: "The constitution does not allow more than one Prime

Minister. For years, I have been groomed to be anointed as the PM. What would happen to my yearning, my ambition, my long outstanding neural-itch, if each Chief Minister becomes the PM.?" Rani Romana assuaged his feelings: "Let us not be perturbed by an unforeseen predicament. When we come to power, we would amend the constitution." Sharda Pawarlekar got up from his chair, elated and gratified: "Let Rani Sahiba explain in detail the plan she has in her mind."

Rani Romana: "When we reach the pinnacle of the political ladder, we can and will amend the constitution. All the Chief Ministers of states will be redesignated as Prime Ministers. A provision will be embedded in the amended constitution that the state Prime Ministers will be immune from any predictable action by anti-graft agencies. And that they will not be hauled up for any act of corruption, such as land scam, mining scam, liquor scam, or any other scam." Then Hello Ram enquired: "And what about defrauding the banks, the government exchequer, pocketing cut money from various infrastructure and welfare projects, etc?"

Rani Romana was ready with the solution: The state Prime Ministers will not be charged for any fraud, any scam, or any loot. They will be allowed to defraud the government coffers, as also the public at large."

Jagdish Babu: "Rani Sahiba! Well said! This is an excellent proposal. But what about the court cases some political leaders, including the ministers and Chief Ministers, are facing?"

Rani Romana: "For this, I too have a strategy up my sleeves. We will pass a law in the Parliament, and withdraw all cases from the courts, and provide the so-called "culprits" the essential relief. I am sure all of you are now satisfied and happy."

Hello Ram: There remains yet another impediment.

Rani Romana: And what is that?

Hello Ram: "People need a Prime Minister to run the country. How can we overcome this problem?"

Rani Romana: There is a simple solution to this riddle. In the amended constitution, we will put in place a plural Executive. That means there will be a Prime Minister in-chief for the purpose of Defence, Finance, Communication, and diplomatic errands. And that Prime Minister in-chief will rotate every two years. Thus, in due course, every state PM will get an opportunity to become the PM-in-chief. Jagdish Babu, fully appeased, announced: This ticklish problem is also solved. I can also aspire to become the PM one day."

All the hundred-odd leaders who had assembled for the conclave cried "hurrah" in unison. They jumped and danced in glee. There was an environment of exultation. There came a garrulous shout: "Hell with ED, CBI, etc. Hail the law of immunity!" But there are still some misgivings and apprehensions. The sceptics feared that the common populace would not accept this type of blanket immunity to the corrupt politicians. Sharda Pawarlekar, a mercurial politician, always changing stand, postulated and advocated: "Politics is the art of the possible. We can make people happy by vain hope. At the time of elections, we all will announce that their government will give free power, free water, free gas cylinders, free bus and rail travel, free ration, and a handsome sum every month to the unemployed, women and poor denizens. These freebies will be sufficiently attractive allurements to lure the common people, and vote for us."

At this point, the foxy Jagdish Babu interjected: "The purported freebies will empty the government coffers. No money will be left for development, for buying the defence equipment, and even for paying the salaries. The country may go bankrupt. Mehul Wangchuck set the scepticism at rest: "I am in the process of inventing a machine with the help of my friends in China. The said project envisages: 'Put potatoes into the machine from one side, and from the other side will come out gold chips.' In due course, the country will amass a lot of gold to make up the loss on account of the freebies." "This is a consoling and heartening project, a unique one. If this project succeeds, Mehul will become the Prime Minister on popular demand," asserted Hello Ram, a Chamcha (spoon) of Rani Romana.

Rani Romana made yet another political revelation: "Since a politician never believes what he says, he is surprised when the common people believe him. One cannot adopt politics as a profession and remain honest. These lollypops will only be a political stratagem to win over the electorates. Once we win and assume power, we know how to hoodwink the populace". Jagdish Babu asked: "What exactly is the subterfuge, the ruse, to bamboozle the public vis-à-vis the announcement of the freebies?" Rani Romana announced: "That is easily done. After we assume the power, we will tell the electorates that a committee, headed by a retired Supreme Court judge, has been formed to work out the pros and cons of the freebies. The committee will take about a year to submit the report. When the report comes, we will reject it, pointing out that in the said report cons are more than the pros. Then we will set up another committee of economists and financial experts. This committee will take a sufficiently long time in submitting the report. Then we will follow yet another ruse to delude the unwary common people. And then we will have the proposed project of Mehul to depend on."

Hello Ram pointed out that "hoodwinking the electorates for five years seemed to be impractical and unworkable a proposal. If our government failed to implement the promises, there would be vociferous criticism from the opposition, and this might result in general unrest." Rani Romana was ready with the solution to this predicament also. She said: "I know how to tackle the uncanny political situation. We will grant some freebees which do not entail much expenditure. This will reassure the common populace that slowly and gradually other promises will also be fulfilled."

Verily, it was just a long-winded discussion, a mere verbosity. Nothing concrete came out of the colloquy. Finally, it was decided to meet again after a month to give a final shape to the alliance and its political agenda. Satyarthi got fed up with the tall talk. He expected that something tangible would emerge out of the conclave and that given his biodata, he would be nominated as the candidate for the Prime Ministership. But that did not happen. Rather the political leaders attending the meeting vied with each other to be "selected" as the prospective candidate for the Prime Ministership. Thus, balked, discontented, and despondent, Satyarthi left the meeting in a huff, boarded a plane, and reached homesick and tired.

Mange Ram announced with finality that ever since Netaji returned from the political conclave, his health started deteriorating. Neither did he eat well, nor could he sleep well. The conclave was marked by hullabaloo, ear-piercing verbal shrieks. The meeting, both times, concluded sans any outcome. This factum situation led to the depression and disappointment of Netaji.

After having heard the full case history of the malady, Dr Daya Ram prescribed some tests. He requested Savitri to get them done and show the report to him. However, Savitri informed that it was only last week that Netaji had got his full body checkup. His head X-ray was also done. Daya Ram asked: "Why did you feel the need for this body check-up and head X-ray?" Savitri replied that a couple of months ago, he had met with an accident, in which his leg was fractured. The political leaders opposed to him declared: "Now with the broken leg he would not be able to contest the election. It is a salubrious augury that he is now out of the race for the post of the PM." Daya Ram desired that the X-ray be shown to him. Savitri brought the X-ray. The doctor looked at it keenly again and again. Then he said that he had never seen such an unusual X-ray before. "There is nothing in his head." Following this investigation, the doctor checked his own blood pressure and found it very high. He immediately gobbled an anti-blood-pressure pill with a glass of water.

Savitri informed the doctor that Netaji frequently suffered fits of tantrums, hoping against hope that he would become the PM. But, in actuality, when his dream of becoming the PM did not materialise, then the sporadic spasm became a regular feature. "He suffers frequent bouts of delirium. When he lost the last election, he quite often bellowed in his sleep: "I have become the Prime Minister. I will take oath tomorrow." With every passing day, his mental condition worsened. "Here he is now in that delirious condition."

Daya Ram: I have now understood the malady and the origin of it. He suffers from a disease called PM-phobia. There are many other regional and national politicians, who too are racked by this epidemic. It may preferably be called the political epidemic. It is a mental malaise; it has no cure. Savitri Madam, please tell Netaji's followers and hangers-on to humour him that he was going to be anointed as the PM in the next election. Thus, the illusionary mirage, the fantasy, will keep his malady in check. And if he is still not cured, the only remedy will be to get him admitted in Marg-Darshak Mandal." After prescribing this panacea for the political disorder, called PM-phobia, the doctor sauntered out.

An appraisal of the political malady will authenticate that a politician is such a flying bird that he can perch on any tree. And if it is a fruit tree, then it is all the more rewarding, nay, profitable. Such flying birds, qua Netas of varied hues and colours, have only one aim in life, and that is to satiate the hunger for dirty lucre. It is for this gainful employment that various political parties come together to form an alliance.

Such a league comprises mausam vigyanik, who can read the vagaries of the political weather, and accordingly change their loyalties. In yester-years, such politicians were called "Aya Ram and Gaya Ram." Now they are nicknamed as *"Paltooram."* They are specialists in hit-and-run. They are, in fact, *parjivi* (rapacious predators). Obviously, such alliances of heterogeneous, diverse political outfits, are formed to win the elections, with the aim to pilfer government treasury and indulge in corrupt practices, scams and frauds to amass wealth. The mirage of motley alliances, eventually, revels in the political circus of filthy and sullied games, and in the process defiles the welfare schemes of the common populace. Such leagues resort to caste politics and play dubious tactics and manoeuvres to dodge and loot the country. The need of the hour is to be wary of such negative politics.

CHAPTER XXXIII

When Thakurji Appears as Witness

In a certain village, there lived a poor farmer, named Kundan. He owned a small piece of land, about two acres, which he tilled to make both ends meet. But he always remained from hand to mouth. Yet he was happy with whatever state he was in, for he was a highly religious, a staunch devotee of Lord Krishna, called Thakurji in local parlance. There was a small temple in front of his house, which he visited regularly to propitiate Thakurji. He would stand in front of the idol of Lord Krishna, qua Thakurji, twice a day, in the morning as also in the evening, and sought the deity's blessings and benedictions. Owing to his devotion for the Supreme Lord, he had calm of mind, and was quite satisfied with his life. He never moaned, never grumbled for his destitution, for Thakurji lived in his heart. Thakurji was his only strength, his only refuge, his only friend in trouble. Verily God chastens the man He loves. And this was so with Kundan. Faith was the only succour he relied on. Faith and prayers were the substitutes for his penury.

Kundan had two sons and one daughter. His daughter was the eldest among his three children. As years passed, his daughter came of age. His wife Anasuya entreated and coaxed him to find a suitable boy for her marriage. In the adjoining village, there lived a small trader, named Raghav, who had a marriageable son. Kundan called on him with the marriage proposal. Raghav agreed to the proposed match. Kundan's daughter was engaged to Raghav's son. Soon a date for the nuptial was fixed. Kundan needed money to perform the marriage of his daughter. Anasuya suggested to him to approach Rupa, the village money lender, and borrow the required money from him.

The next morning Kundan visited Rupa and requested him to lend him the pecuniary assistance for his daughter's marriage. Rupa agreed. But he stipulated a condition that for the loan Kundan should pledge his land to him. "When you pay off your debt with 15 percent interest, I will release your land, and give it back to you. And if you fail to pay back the loaned money, I will confiscate your land," Rupa foisted the condition. Since necessity is the mother of invention, the force of necessity is irresistible. Kundan signed the bond, collected the sum he needed, and returned home. He solemnised the marriage of his daughter on the due date.

Years passed. Kundan's sons, diligent and intelligent, completed their education, and eventually got lucrative jobs. They were highly obedient and dutiful young boys and were devoted to their father. By dint of hard work, they earned and saved a lot of money. One day, the duo asked their father to pay off the debt to the money lender, and get the mortgaged land released. Kundan called on Rupa the next day, returned the loaned money with interest, and beseeched him to release the pledged land. Rupa brought the agreement signed by Kundan. He also wrote a receipt for the money having been paid in full with interest and asked Kundan to read it and append his signatures on it. But Kundan said: "I am an illiterate person, I can neither read nor write. I will put my thumb impression."

Suddenly Rupa thought of chicanery, of double-dealing. He took the paper back from the hands of Kundan, went in, and prepared another document, and asked Kundan to append his thumb impression on it, which the unlettered farmer did. He did not have any inkling, nor any suspicion, that the money-lender would hoodwink him. Rupa had played a mischief. He had altered the document. On the "fresh' document he had written that Kundan had paid a part of the debt, and that "so much" money was still left to be paid with interest, and that the pledged land would be returned after the entire sum had been paid.

Kundan, the unwary farmer, sauntered back home, satisfied and stress-free. Years passed. Rupa filed a complaint in a court of law for the recovery of the balance amount. The court issued summons to him. Kundan appeared before the judge on the stipulated date.

Judge: Kundan. You owe a lot of money to Rupa. And if you don't pay it, your land will be confiscated.

Kundan: My Lord! I have paid the entire amount with interest, and I don't owe even a penny to him.

Rupa: Sir, he is lying. Here is the paper with his thumb impression in which he has admitted that he owes money, and would pay it later on.

Judge: Kundan, you say that you have paid the entire sum, but the money-lender says that you still have to pay a lot of money to him. And in support of his averment, he has produced a paper signed by you. Do you have any witness to corroborate what you aver?

Kundan: Yes Sir. I paid the entire money with interest in the presence of Thakurji. Thakurji is my only witness.

The Judge ordered his minions to issue summons to Thakurji to appear in the court on the next date. The court officials, with the summons in hand, searched every nook and corner of the village, including the temple, but they could not find any person with the name of Thakurji. Rupa was highly pleased. He thought that he would win the case, as there did not exist any person with the name of Thakurji in the entire village.

On the next date of the hearing, the court officials shouted *"Thakurji hazir ho!"* Suddenly, an old man, bearded with matted hair, clad in a saffron dress, looking like a mendicant, nay a sage, appeared and stood before the judge.

Judge: Old man, what do you know about this case?

Old Man: Kundan had paid the entire amount in my presence. He owes nothing to Rupa.

Rupa: Sir, here is the paper on which Kundan had acknowledged that he owed money to me. Here he has appended his thumb impression.

Judge: Respected saint. This paper tells a different story.

Old Man: No sir. This is not the real document. Rupa is telling a lie, for he has played a fraud on Kundan

Judge: Then where is the real document?

Old Man: The original document, the real one, is lying hidden in the house of Rupa. The money-lender has three almirahs, marked one, two, and three, placed in the basement of his dwelling. In the almirah number three, there is a file of blue colour lying on the middle shelf of the cupboard. On page 22 of that file, the original document is placed. On this document is written that Kundan has paid the entire amount and that he owes nothing to Rupa. Please send your officials to search Rupa's house, and get that file.

The judge ordered his officials to go to Rupa's house and bring that file. The file was brought and produced before the Judge. The purported document clinched the issue. The Judge ordered that Kundan did not owe any money to Rupa and that he had paid the entire sum. He reprimanded Rupa for misleading the court and sent him to prison for deceit, duplicity and lying.

The judge stood up. And so did all those present in the court. He wanted to bow before the saffron-clad sadhu. But the sage was nowhere to be seen. People ran here and there to locate him, but he had gone. Nobody knew as to from where he had come, and to which place he had gone. The wise judge understood that it was indeed Thakurji who had come Himself to depose as a witness and help his devotee (bhakta). The judge relinquished his post. He wandered from temple to temple to expiate, to atone for the sin he had committed by making Thakurji stand in his presence in his court.

The judge was convinced that what happened in his court was a miracle. He felt that faith could make miracles happen. For, God never lets his devotee down; He reciprocates the devotee's faith, the devotee's confidence.

CHAPTER XXXIV

Cat Scan

A rustic woman, an affluent one, lived on her agricultural farm, situated in the suburb of a town. She was a lover of flora and fauna. Besides having milch-animals, she had some ducks, which frolicked and cackled in the spacious compound of her farmhouse.

One day, one of the ducks met with an accident. Her leg was hurt and she limped. She appeared to be too sick to survive. The woman took the bird to a veterinary surgeon for treatment. The vet laid the bird on the table, took out his stethoscope, and listened to the heat-beat of the duck. He indulged in this exercise for a little while. Then he rolled his eyes, looked towards the lady, and shook his head. With gloom writ large on his face, he said: "Dear lady! Your duck is dead."

The woman felt morose. She did not believe the vet. She said: "Doctor, are you sure that the duck has passed away." The vet replied: "Yes, I am sure that the bird is no more." "How can you be so sure," the woman protested. "You have not done any testing on her. She might just be in a coma, or slightly unconscious."

The vet turned around and went inside a room. A few minutes later, he came back with a Labrador. The rustic woman looked at the vet and the dog in amazement. The dog stood on the hind legs, put his front paws on the examination table, and sniffed the duck literally from top to toe. The lady asked: "Doctor, what are you doing?" The vet replied, "Dogs have a great sense of smell which helps them discover different objects, and provide essential information. Therefore, the dog will find out as to what is wrong with the duck."

The dog smelt the bird, looked up at the vet, and shook its head. The vet understood the beastly lingua franca. He dragged the dog by the leash and sauntered back to the room he had emerged with Lab-ra-dor. A few minutes later, the vet returned. This time with a cat. The cat jumped on the table, delicately sniffed the bird from head to toe, mewed a little, and sat back on its haunches. The cat, like the dog, shook its head, wagged its tail, and softly strolled out of the examination room. The vet with eyes downcast, and slightly crestfallen, looked into the eyes of the woman and reiterated: "I am sorry, madam. As I opined earlier, your duck is dead. I can certifiably and definitely say that the duck is no more."

Then, the vet moved to the computer table, turned the computer on, and produced a bill, which he handed over to the lady. The rustic woman, still in shock, took the bill. She cried: "Three-thousand rupees! Just to tell me that my duck is dead." The vet blinked his eyes, smiled a little, and shrugged his shoulders: "Madam! If you had accepted my word in the beginning that the duck was dead, the bill would have been just Rs. 100. But with the Lab (Lab-ra-dor) report, and "cat scan," it is now 3000. It is your fault, not mine. You insisted on a thorough examination of the sick bird, which I did. You must bear the brunt. The rustic woman paid the hefty amount and walked out of the vet's room grumbling and vilifying the crooked veterinary surgeon.

CHAPTER XXXV

Of Pencil and Eraser

I am a pencil. I have a long history. I owe my genesis, my emergence, into the world, to an ancient Roman writing instrument, called stylus used in writing on clay, or waxed tablets. Scribes used this metal rod to leave a readable mark on papyrus (*Bhojpatra, an early form of paper*). Subsequently, styluses were made of lead, which is what we call pencil cores. Over the centuries, I have evolved to the present mould and shape, and have come of age. I have become what I am. I am made of slats (thin narrow pieces of wood), which form the outer cover. And what is important is what is there inside me. The school-going children use me to learn and write numbers in their mathematic notebooks. Even the adolescent college-going students, the professors, the professionals, and the scribes, can't do without me.

There is no gainsaying the fact that the old-timers held me in their hands with pride and reverence, and often with a smile. It was the best of times when having me in the writing kit, was considered to be a luxury. Then I was less in demand. But now my demand is much higher, as millions of students are back in schools, attending classes in person.

I have always been easily available then and now. I did not, and do not, cost much. Not long ago, there was a lead of black colour inserted inside me. Now I am available in many colours. Yet my demand in the original colour, that is black, is intact.

Significantly, I remain insufficient, nay deficient, sans eraser. I am coupled with it. Eraser is my ally and helpmate. Whenever I make a mistake, the eraser is always there to erase it and make my mistake vanish away. In the process, my friend eraser gets hurt owing to me, and loses a part of itself, and gets smaller each time. However, the eraser is very generous and munificent. It always avers: "Pencil! My dear friend. It is true that I lose a part of myself every time I am used to remove the mistake you make. I know that eventually I would be gone. But I don't mind. I was made to do this. Therefore, worry you not. I will not be happy to see you sad."

I am symptomatic of five things which each pencil-holder must know, and needs to know about me:

1. I need to be remembered always. Let no one be oblivious to me.
2. I am like a man who is the creation of God. Like man, what is important in me, is what is inside me. A man sans soul is lifeless, is cipher. Similarly, what is inside me, is the most valued.
3. On every surface, I am used, I leave my mark. No matter what the condition may be, I must continue to write, good, bad or worse. And so are the known or unknown, written or unwritten actions of man.

(4) I have a purpose in my heart. I understand and promise to remember what went inside me.

(5) I am blessed with many gifts and talents, which enable me to accomplish many appreciable and momentous things, provided I am held in someone's hands. Similarly, man is capable of doing many great errands, temporal, spiritual and psychological, if only he allows himself to be handled by Perfect Hands.

I experience powerful sharpening from time to time. But this unpleasant, agonising suffering, is essential to become better and smoother. And I am able to correct my mistakes with the help of an Eraser.

Please replace me with you as an individual. Remember the advice and never forget it, and thus you too will become the best person in the world. You will be able to do many great things, but only if you allow yourself to be held in God's hands. Like me, you must allow other human beings to access the many gifts and talents you possess. You will experience powerful sharpening from time to time by going through many trials and tribulations. You need each sharpening to make yourself stronger and smoother and a better person.

You will be able to correct some of the howlers with the help of Eraser and would grow wise through them. The most important part of you is what is inside you, that is your soul. On every surface on which you walk, you must leave your mark, your footprints. No matter what the situation is, you must thank your Creator in everything you do. And, thus, you make Him visible in this world through you.

Not only God, but our parents too, are like erasers. And we are like a pencil. They are always there for their children, cleaning up their mistakes. Sometimes along the way they get hurt, and in the process become smaller. And it is owing to them, their onerous, arduous and gruelling efforts – qua through their sharpening that we ultimately get repaired, rectified, and ameliorated.

CHAPTER XXXVI

Charity Begins at Tree

Rishi, a teacher in a school, was walking back home after the day's work. On the way he espied a paper hung on the trunk of a tree with something written on it in bold letters. He sauntered close to the tree, and perused what was written on the paper: "I lost a fifty-rupee note while passing through this way yesterday. I am an aged woman. I have weak eyesight; I cannot see properly. Whosoever finds that note, please return the same at the address given below."

Reading that leaflet, the kind-hearted teacher decided to go to the aged lady at the given address. He walked towards her house, situated at the end of a narrow lane. He knocked at the door, and shouted: "Is there anybody inside?" Soon an old woman, decrepit and debilitated, walking with the help of a stick, came out. As she could hardly see, she tottered while walking.

She asked: "Who are you, son? And what brings you here? I am in the evening of my life. There is nobody to look after me. I live in this house alone." Rishi, as implied in his name, a saintly person by nature, replied: "Mother! My name is Rishi. I am a teacher. I have found the fifty-rupee note you lost on the way. I have come to deliver it to you."

Hearing this, tears wallowed in the eyes of the aged woman. She said: "Son! Till now more than fifty persons have called on me, each giving a fifty-rupee note to me. I am unlettered. I can neither read nor write. I cannot see properly. I don't know who is that philanthropic person who wrote and hung that handbill on the tree. Obviously, that munificent person took pity on my condition. And in order to help me, he resorted to that charitable act.

Nevertheless, the aged lady kept the note on the repeated insistence of Rishi. She, however, said: "Son! I have neither written nor hung that paper. Obviously, it is the handiwork of some noble soul. Nonetheless, while going back, please remove that paper, tear it into shreds, and throw it away." The teacher said: "Yes, I would do that." But the human soul inside the teacher compelled and impelled him to ruminate that the "aged mother" must have said the same thing to everybody who called on her with the fifty-rupee note. But nobody tore the paper away.

What is right and what is wrong, only two people know: God and the soul inside the human being. The heart of Rishi overflowed with a sense of gratitude for the man who did that yeoman deed, wrote that pamphlet and hung it at the tree trunk. Verily, there are many ways to help the needy, and offer fiscal assistance, but this kind of device to help the old and crippled woman, was a unique gesture, a heart-touching feat.

Rishi, the teacher, did not tear that paper, for he believed that helping some destitute, willy-nilly, was an altruistic and righteous act. "One must follow the path of magnanimity and big-heartedness," would be the message of the noble soul.

CHAPTER XXXVII

Money Speaks

This is the story of Visnu Sharma. Not that historical Vishnu Sharma who wrote *Panchtantra*, but an ordinary mortal. Owing to the resemblance of his name with that of historical Vishnu Sharma, he was jocularly referred as Panchtantra Maharaj. And when people greeted him as such, he always smiled ebulliently, and so did those who called him by this nomenclature. He has all the positive and negative idiosyncrasies, flaws and faults of a pulsating human being. In fact, his life has been a journey, willy-nilly, from being to becoming.

Vishnu Sharma has been an ordinary being, like any one of us, getting up early in the morning, going for a stroll, gossiping and giggling with his co-walkers, and cutting jokes. Such has been the lively beginning of his day. After finishing his morning chores, he regularly visited the temple, situated just in front of his house, paid obeisance and oblations to Lord Krishna. He was, obviously, a highly religious person, given to spiritual pursuits. For any and every errand, he invariably invoked Lord Krishna and sought His backing and approval. For him, Krishna was his Bhagwan, his inner voice, the voice of his Atma (soul).

Vishnu Sharma was a money lender. He lent money to the needy on interest. So, in a way, he was a friend in need, a friend indeed. Most of his clients were "small" people, petty shopkeepers, street vendors, or those who needed money for socio-religious ceremonies. He kept the complete record of the borrowers in his *Bahi* (ledger), such as Ram Lal, son of Shyam Lal, who borrowed so much money, etc. Over the years he had amassed a lot of black money, which he had invested in the share-market. Notwithstanding his having garnered dirty lucre by means fair and foul, he always gave credit to Lord Krishna for all the money he earned. Since he invoked Krishna every day for two hours in the temple, he felt that God was always kind to him and that He was always on his side.

The black money with him proliferated. He wanted to invest it in some venture. He, however, left the decision to the will of God. He thought that he would embark on some lucrative business when Bhagwan Krishna so determined. One day after the pooja in the temple, he stood before the deity with folded hands: "My Lord Krishna! I have collected a lot of wealth. Please advise me, nay command me, as to what should I do with this money. Please show me the way. Bestow your benediction on me."

The response to his prayer, there came a voice from the void. It was perhaps his inner voice: "You fool! Despite your having hoarded huge wealth, you do not know how and where to invest it." Vishnu said: "Bhagwan Ji! I am a simpleton. I need your guidance." Bhagwan, qua Krishna, proposed: "Why don't you open a hotel? These days hotel business is a highly remunerative and profit-making enterprise." Vishnu considered the advice of his Bhagwan, deemed it as the commandment of Lord Krishna, and opened a hotel, a big one, in the posh area of the town. The hotel had highly garnished rooms, well-furnished washrooms, and highly attractive interior and exterior. The hotel had all other facilities: a laundry, a barber shop, a taxi stand, a spacious lawn and a terrace garden. Since Vishnu was a devout brahmin, he decided to provide only the vegetarian food. Soon the business boomed. It was visited by big business-houses, which held meetings and conferences there. And many senior bureaucrats also thronged in the hotel. Vishnu was elated to see the hotel flourishing and thriving.

One day some customers approached Vishnu with the complaint: "In such a posh hotel, the patrons are served only the vegetarian food. Why don't you supply non-vegetarian food? We will go to some other hotel next time if you fail to make arrangements for the non-vegetarian fare." Vishnu replied: "I am a brahmin, a Vaishnav, and a devotee of Lord Krishna. How can I supply meat in my hotel? I am a highly religious person. Your demand poses a great conscientious dilemma. It hurts the morale and morality of a devout brahmin." The customers said: "Since you are a Vaishnav, you ought to have opened a road-side Dhaba instead of a hotel. None will stay in your hotel in future. We too are in the business. We do not follow dharma always, nor you do. None can vouch for dharma while in business, particularly when one is in the hotel business."

Vishnu found himself between the devil and the deep sea. Nevertheless, he decided to ask Lord Krishna, his Bhagwan, his mentor and guide. He stood before the idol of his Bhagwan, and supplicated: "Prabhu, the customers demand non-veg food. Lord, you know I am a Vaishnav. How can I supply mutton, chicken, fish, etc? And if I do not acquiesce and yield before their demand, my business will go to dogs. It is you, my Lord, who has given this hotel to me. Please show me the way out of this quandary, otherwise I will go bankrupt." Then came out the same inner voice of his soul: "You dunce! You blockhead! Why don't you realise the discomfort, the twinge of your clients when they do not get the food of their taste and liking? Understand their need, their taste-buds, and satisfy the tang of their palate, and provide non-veg food."

Vishnu understood the "intention" of Bhagwan Ji. He ordered his minions to supply non-veg fare, mutton, chicken, and fish to the patrons in the hotel. Eventually, his clientele increased. His business swelled. However, one day a senior Executive of a big corporate house called on Vishnu with the proposal of his company that his company would hold an annual meeting in the hotel. Vishnu presented the menu card and furnished other details of the facilities. The business executive, after scanning through the menu and rate card, was satisfied that the hotel provided the non-veg food. He then asked: "What about the arrangements to "digest" such spicy and tangy food?" Vishnu replied: "There is no problem. The hotel management will provide Hazmola, an Ayurvedic concoction to help digest/ absorb, the non-veg food." The Executive shook his head in exasperation: "Not the digestive tablets or *churan*. I mean something more potent, that is wine and beer." Vishnu scratched his head: "Sir, there are no arrangements for alcohol. I can make available *charnamrit*, the holy water prepared by the temple priest. But no liquor." The Executive said: "In that eventuality, we will hold the annual meeting in some other hotel, or guest house." "Please don't take a decision in a hurry. Let me consult Krishna, my guide and philosopher, and seek his permission for the supply of liquor. If my Bhagwan agrees, I will supply wine and beer. Please wait till tomorrow morning," pleaded Vishnu

The next morning Vishnu again approached Lord Krishna in the temple and supplicated: "Lord, the customers have now demanded liquor. How can I provide wine and beer?" Then came the voice from the void as usual: "You ninny! Don't you know that the demigods drank Somrus, which was a form of alcohol? Where does your Vaishnav dharma come in between you and your business? In verse 63 of the Sam Veda, Somrus, that is liquor, has been eulogised. It seems apparent that you do not have any scriptural knowledge; you obviously lack intellect and comprehension about things ancient." Vishnu understood the mandate of Bhagwan. He opened a bar in the hotel. The hotel business further proliferated. However, one day a foreign delegation came to the hotel. They took the details of the menu and other facilities. They were pleased that the Hotel provided non-veg food, wine and beer, as also many other facilities. So, the foreigners decided to stay at the hotel. In the evening, the leader of the delegation, in a hush-hush voice, mumbled in undertones: "The hotel provided non-veg food, wine and beer. But what about the "live meat?" "What is that?" asked Vishnu. The foreigner said: "I mean cabaret, in which young women dance half-naked or fully naked." Vishnu chanted: "Radhe, Radhe! What nonsense?" The foreigner retorted: "There is nothing surprising, unusual, or wrong. In every hotel, there are arrangements for cabaret dancers."

Vishnu said: "I am a staunch (*kutter*) Vaishnav. Nevertheless, I will place your demand before Bhagwan Krishna." The next day, he again pleaded before Krishna: "Lord, the customers, especially the foreign ones, want cabaret dance in the hotel, that is young women dancing half or fully naked." Promptly came the voice from the void (obviously his inner voice): "Fool! Don't you know I am Vishnu, the Supreme God? In my Krishan avatar, I performed *raslila* with Gopis, the cowherdesses. What hesitation do you have in arranging the modern *raslila*?" Following the direction of Bhagwan, Vishnu arranged a cabaret dance in the hotel. Nonetheless, after some days a client asked the bearer: "Is there something "touchable", something entertaining in the hotel?" The bearer asked: "What is that Sir?" "Something "fleshy" to physically entertain, said the client." The bearer replied: "No sir. This does not happen in this hotel." The client went to Vishnu: "Who would stay in this hotel, for there is no arrangement to amuse and enjoy in the night?" Vishnu replied: "For this, there is a cabaret." "Cabaret happens at a distance. I want "something" closer in the bed." Vishnu once again approached Bhagwan Ji. "Sir, the customers now want the supply of women with liquor. How can I commit that sin." The inner voice suggested: "Fool! Male-female cohabitation is the law of the Nature. It is there among birds and beasts, as also among men and women. There is no concept of sin in it. But you must do so clandestinely escaping the prying eyes of the police. And charge 20 per cent extra from such customers." This was, obviously, the voice not of Krishna, but of his conscience gone awry, the conscience which no longer pricked his soul. Vishnu accepted the demand. The hotel ran by leaps and bounds. Obviously, dharma was hooked with business. Dharma or no dharma, business and sin are inter-connected, are complementary and supplementary to each other.

There is no gainsaying the fact that: "Money speaks, money reigns, and money does everything." This aphorism stands corroborated and substantiated by the story of Vishnu Sharma. Verily, one who makes haste to be rich, cannot be innocent, because the love of money is the root of all evil. For people like Vishnu and his ilk, money is like the sixth sense without which they cannot adhere to the use of the other five. Eventually, what happened is a lesson for all of us. Obviously, money can buy the people of the earth, but not the denizens of the other world. When the "time" comes, the messengers of Death cannot wait; they cannot be bought with dirty lucre. With tears of repentance and remorse in his eyes, Vishnu departed from this world. Verily, the desire to get rich quickly makes one oblivious to the value of time. Money may buy anything and everything, but it cannot buy time. At long last, the Death takes the corporeal breath away.

About The Book

A parable is a short story that illustrates a moral attitude, or a religious principle. Stories, by and large, fall into three categories: Temporal, spiritual and psychological. Secular stories, or tales, embody secular (temporal) literature, while the spiritual literature encompasses socio-religious and didactic tales. And then there are psychological stories. The Hindi equivalent of literature is Sahitya. Sahitya is of two types: *Swanta sukhaiy*, and *Parjan Hitaiy*. *Swanta sukhaiy* is the sahitya, qua literature, that is produced for self-delight, self-pleasure and self-satisfaction, while *parjan hitaiy* sahitya has wider connotations; it affects the manners and the morals, and is prone to bring about a salubrious transformation in human conduct and idiosyncrasies. Parables, that is the didactic literature, fall in this category. Therefore, efforts have been made to Include parables, and other didactic stories, in this book: they will, willy-nilly, refine the sensibilities of the people at large.

About The Author

Dr. C. D. Verma

Dr C. D. VERMA is a former Associate Professor and Head, Department of English, Hans Raj College, University of Delhi. During his long teaching career, he has written a number of books. His books, *The Reverberations of Gita* in *World Literature, The Exile Hero and the Reintegrating Vision, W.H.Auden: Selected Poems, Look Back in Anger, and Mrs. Dalloway,* have been widely acclaimed. His latest books include *The Sermons in Stones, Something to Crow About, Know the Seers of India, Renowned Sages of Ancient India, The Story Time, Recalling Epic Tales from Ramayana and Mahabharata:* these books have been published by Amazon (Notion Press).

www.ingramcontent.com/pod-product-compliance
Lightning Source LLC
Chambersburg PA
CBHW031133130726
47988CB00006B/2356